GREATEST ELK

A COMPLETE HISTORICAL AND
ILLUSTRATED RECORD OF
NORTH AMERICA'S BIGGEST ELK

BY

ROGER SELNER

SAFARI PRESS INC.

The trademark Safari Press ® is registered with the U.S. Patent and Trademark Office and in other countries.

Selner, Roger

First edition

Safari Press Inc.

2001, Long Beach, California

ISBN 1-57157-210-4

Library of Congress Catalog Card Number: 00-101829

10 9 8 7 6 5 4 3 2 1

Readers wishing to receive the Safari Press catalog, featuring many fine books on big-game hunting, wingshooting, and sporting firearms, should write to Safari Press Inc., P.O. Box 3095, Long Beach, CA 90803, USA. Tel: (714) 894-9080 or visit our Web site at www.safaripress.com.

DEDICATION

Dedicated to Jean and Orville Norman, my mom and dad, for taking me
fishing and hunting and for allowing me to grow up in the outdoors.

In memory of my father, who passed away in 1992. He
would have enjoyed this book.

TABLE OF CONTENTS

TABLE OF CONTENTS (CONTINUED)

TABLE OF CONTENTS (CONTINUED)

FOREWORD

Anyone who loves reading about hunting elk, especially trophy elk, will be delighted with this book. Roger Selner has left no stone unturned in seeking the stories and photos of the biggest bulls ever taken. It's obvious that Roger has a passion for enormous elk. I've known him for many years, and have seen his intense devotion when it comes to researching and tracking down rumors of huge bulls. Like a hound dog on a hot trail, Roger pursues his leads until he finally comes up with the bull in question.

This book shows, in stunning color photos, more than forty of the biggest bulls ever taken anywhere. As a bonus, you'll read how many of the bulls were taken, as well as how they were discovered. Many of them turned up in garages, attics, and dusty basements. Roger has researched each bull's history and includes here the little details that make for fascinating reading.

There are individual stories by hunters telling how they found their trophies, from the beginning of the trail to the final shot. You'll feel their excitement and other emotions as they walked up to their prize, profoundly amazed at the size of the body and the reach of the horns.

The mix of trophy elk pictured in this book is incredible, from bulls with the most points, to elk with palmated racks and bizarre growths, to photos of giant sheds, many of them from elk that could still be roaming the forests today.

Roger Selner has done a magnificent job in creating a masterpiece. The bulls pictured here defy the imagination, and this book is a work of art that deserves to be treasured in every elk hunter's library.

Jim Zumbo
Hunting Editor, *Outdoor Life*
Cody, Wyoming
February 2000

ACKNOWLEDGMENTS

I want to thank Safari Press and Ludo Wurfbain for their assistance and encouragement in creating this book.

I am grateful to my wife, Karen, for living with me and tolerating all the conversations about hunting, antlers, trophies, and record heads, as well as the many memories that adorn our walls.

Special Thanks To:
Don Stemler for all the help and the many miles we put in together traveling the country and his wealth of information on trophy heads.

Extended Thanks To:
Mike and Bertie Eastman
Eastmans' Hunting Journal
Jerry Brekke, Brekke Photography
Jim Zumbo
Jack Reneau

Hunters and Trophy Owners:

Sam Aho	Lou A. DePaolis
John Antonio	Keith Dunbar
Bass Pro Wildlife Museum	Brady J. Dupke
Sean Burdeniuk	Alan Ellsworth
James R. Berry	John Fitchett
Dan Boles	Kevin Fugere
Nathaniel Boni	Grant Garcia
Ernie Bernat	Bill Hamilton
Harold and Belva Burroughs	Dana Hollinger
Marshall Bylas	Bob Howard
Brian Clark	Frank Hudson
Terry V. Crooks	Ron Hulse
Steve Crossley	Joe Jessel

ACKNOWLEDGMENTS (CONTINUED)

Reed and Shirley Johnson
The Lamb Family
Kurt Ludlow
Mark Martin
Fred and Maxine Mercer
Mannie Moore
Rod M. Odenbach
Tim Pender
Mike Rodgers
Ed Rozman
San Carlos Apache Tribe
Tom Satre
Joe Schaefer

Fred Scott
Gerald Small
Warren and Jenny Spriggs
Steve Stevens
Billy Stockton
Rick Stone
Warren Stone
Rex and Terri Summerfield
Arlan W. Tift
Todd and Julia Troy
Chris White
Shawn White
Guy Woods

North American Records Organizations:
Boone and Crockett Club
Pope and Young Club
Longhunter Club
North American Shed Hunters Club

Taxidermists:
Jim Brandenburg
Hayes-Niemeyer
Scott Lennard
John Lewton
Gerry Mercer
Dennis Shoemaker
Philip Soucy

ACKNOWLEDGMENTS (CONTINUED)

My Many Friends Who Helped with Input, Information, and Photos:
Jeff and Becky Barber
Bass Pro Shops
Randy Bean
Brent Fitchett
Bill Harlan
Rich Hayes
Randy Higley
Jeff Hints
Fred King
Doug Lobaugh
Rainbow Enterprises
Realtree Outdoor Products
James Ritchie
Tim and Kathy Robertson
Rocky Mountain Elk Foundation
Greg and Darlene Smith
Trophy Hunters magazine
Mac Vosbeck
Gary Wise
Paul Wolterbeek

. . . and many others whom I unintentionally have forgotten to thank.

INTRODUCTION

My interest in antlers started more than forty years ago when I bought my first Boone & Crockett record book and a Boone & Crockett book on measuring and scoring big-game trophies. I have been studying and collecting record books since then, and I am currently an official measurer for Boone & Crockett, Pope and Young, and Longhunters clubs.

I enjoy measuring trophies for people, but what really got me excited was hearing all the old stories, looking at the old photos (new ones, too), and watching the excitement on the faces of hunters and their families when, after twenty, forty, or even one hundred years, they find out that their trophy is a record.

My interest in antlers really took off in 1986 when I started traveling with Dick Idol's whitetail collection and later traveled with a mule deer display until 1995.

In 1995 I started the World Record Elk Tour. I wanted people to share in the magnificence of these great trophies and be able to hear the stories behind them. At this writing the tour is entering its seventh year. I have done more than one hundred shows and displayed forty-seven different elk heads. Now in this book I can share with you the photos, the stories, and the score sheets behind each great elk.

Many trophies are entered in the record books, but the *Greatest Elk* goes beyond the record books. Some of these great heads cannot be officially recorded because the skulls are cracked or were cut in half to facilitate packing the heads out of the mountains. Other old heads have fallen off walls and been broken or damaged, but they are great elk nonetheless.

I have mounted shed antlers to create some of the heads in the tour. In several cases, the shed antlers exceed the official records. As you read about the Roosevelt sheds from Oregon, for example, you will learn how the largest set scored forty inches more than the world record. The sheds are proof of the existence of superb animals that were never harvested or found dead.

Nearly every week I get a lead about an old head that hangs on a wall somewhere, resulting in a folder full of potential new records. As I travel coast to coast several times a year, I try to track the leads down. It has become a passion (my wife, Karen, says it's an obsession) of mine to record hunting history while the family members or the hunters themselves still remember the stories, to prevent this lore from becoming lost forever.

One of hunting history's great stops is the Meeker Hotel and Cafe in Meeker, Colorado. The original hotel was built in 1886. Some twenty-five great game heads adorn the walls, and four elk really stand out, as you'll read about in these pages. About half of the old deer mounts had the hunter's license tacked on the back, some dating back to the 1920s.

Not all the great heads in this book have a detailed story. Some chapters merely note when the animal was found dead or where a set of sheds was found. I want to bring these great elk to you through this book and out on the tour as we travel the country. Each elk is unique, and many are nontypical racks with multiple points—standouts when you consider that a normal mature bull elk has six points on each side.

For me, all the great stories and heads, the many people I have met, and the friendships that have evolved make life worth living. During sixteen years on the road, I have covered one million-plus miles, providing 300 shows in 126 different locations across the country.

God made animals for us to enjoy, whether we choose to hunt them, photograph them, or just admire them. With this in mind, I hope you enjoy the *Greatest Elk*.

GREATEST
ELK

CHAPTER 1

WORLD RECORD
TYPICAL
SHEDS

B&C 450 $^6/_8$

BY PAUL WOLTERBEEK

These sheds were found in the Dry Lake region of Arizona's San Carlos Apache Reservation in 1986–87. John Antonio, a tribal member, was hunting deer in the mountains around Dry Lake when he came across a single remarkable antler. *This is pretty huge*, Antonio thought. Since he didn't know anything about world records or elk racks, he just picked it up and brought it back to camp.

Tribal member Marshall Bylas found his half of the world record elk sheds near Dry Lake in the Reservation's Nantac Rim area. He and his partner, Stevenson Talgo, were surveying pine, juniper, and other trees for the Forest Resource Department's inventory program.

"To tell you the truth, I've found quite a few antlers while working for the Forestry Department, but I didn't think much of this one until I heard it was the biggest shed antler," said Bylas.

It was brought to the tribe's wildlife department, where it was matched with the other side. The head is on display at the department.

In the office of the San Carlos Apache Tribe, Arizona.

My good friend Ron Zurek holds the sheds at a taxidermy shop. He is 6 feet, 3 inches tall, so you can see the size of the antlers.

WORLD RECORD TYPICAL SHEDS

Year: 1986/1987

Found by: John Antonio and Marshall Bylas

Location: San Carlos Apache Reservation, Arizona

Owner: San Carlos Apache Tribe

	Typical Points				Nontypical Points	
	Right Antler	Left Antler	Difference		Right Antler	Left Antler
Main Beam Length	56 2/8	57 4/8	1 2/8	1st Point		
1st Point	19 0/8	18 4/8	4/8	2nd Point		
2nd Point	20 2/8	20 3/8	1/8	3rd Point		
3rd Point	15 4/8	14 6/8	6/8	4th Point		
4th Point	20 3/8	21 6/8	1 3/8	5th Point		
5th Point	19 6/8	22 3/8	2 5/8	6th Point		
6th Point	14 2/8	13 0/8	1 2/8	7th Point		
7th Point	4 4/8	5 7/8	1 3/8	8th Point		
8th Point				9th Point		
1st Circumference	10 0/8	9 7/8	1/8	10th Point		
2nd Circumference	9 2/8	8 6/8	4/8	11th Point		
3rd Circumference	6 7/8	7 1/8	2/8	12th Point		
4th Circumference	6 6/8	6 7/8	1/8	13th Point		
				Subtotals		
Total	202 6/8	206 6/8	10 2/8	Total		

DATA		TOTALS	
Number of Points Right	8	Inside Spread	51 4/8
Number of Points Left	8	Right Antler	202 6/8
Total Nontypical	None	Left Antler	206 6/8
Tip to Tip Spread	Unknown	Typical Gross Score	461 0/8
Greatest Spread	55 6/8	Difference	-10 2/8
Inside Spread, Estimated	51 4/8	Typical Net Score	450 6/8
		Nontypical	0
Gross Score	461 0/8	Typical Score	450 6/8

CHAPTER 2

NUMBER 2 WORLD RECORD
TYPICAL
SHEDS

B&C 446 ⁵/₈

This set of sheds has the largest frame of any typical elk, 466 ²/₈ inches, with a conservative inside spread of 45 inches. The right antler measures 210 ⁴/₈ inches and the left 210 ⁶/₈ inches.

The sheds were originally mounted on a skull carved out of a large block of wood. Holes were drilled in each antler, and a long rod was inserted into each to secure it to the block of wood.

The old mount was so small and the rack so big that it fell off the wall numerous times. The antlers have subsequently been repaired and restored.

We are still working to capture more of the history, including who found the sheds and when.

I took photos of the old bull when it hung on the back wall of the Meeker, Colorado, museum. You can see the damaged points and the small old mount. Jeff Hints of Philip Soucy Studios in Libby, Montana, spent many hours restoring the old mount.

This is one of the four largest heads that is still in the Meeker Hotel.

Photo taken in the Meeker Museum shows some of what the heads found there looked like before they were restored.

Meeker Hotel & Cafe, Meeker, Colorado.

NUMBER 2 WORLD RECORD TYPICAL SHEDS

Year: Prior to 1930
Found by: Unknown

Location: Meeker, Colorado area
Owner: Meeker Hotel & Cafe

	Typical Points				Nontypical Points	
	Right Antler	Left Antler	Difference		Right Antler	Left Antler
Main Beam Length	56 5/8	56 0/8	5/8	1st Point	2 0/8	
1st Point	18 7/8	19 2/8	3/8	2nd Point		
2nd Point	18 3/8	16 4/8	1 7/8	3rd Point		
3rd Point	25 0/8	22 0/8	3 0/8	4th Point		
4th Point	24 4/8	24 1/8	3/8	5th Point		
5th Point	17 0/8	18 5/8	1 5/8	6th Point		
6th Point	12 6/8	13 4/8	1 6/8	7th Point		
7th Point	2 0/8	7 3/8	5 3/8	8th Point		
8th Point				9th Point		
1st Circumference	9 6/8	9 4/8	2/8	10th Point		
2nd Circumference	8 0/8	8 0/8	0	11th Point		
3rd Circumference	7 4/8	7 6/8	2/8	12th Point		
4th Circumference	8 0/8	8 1/8	1/8	13th Point		
				Subtotals	2 0/8	
Total	208 4/8	210 6/8	15 5/8	Total	2 0/8	

DATA		TOTALS	
Number of Points Right	9	Inside Spread	45 0/8
Number of Points Left	8	Right Antler	208 4/8
Total Nontypical	2 0/8	Left Antler	210 6/8
Tip to Tip Spread	51 0/8	Typical Gross Score	464 2/8
Greatest Spread	54 0/8	Difference	-15 5/8
Inside Spread, Estimated	45 0/8	Typical Net Score	448 5/8
		Nontypical	-2 0/8
Gross Score	464 2/8	Typical Score	446 5/8

NEW WORLD RECORD
TYPICAL

B&C 442 ⁵/₈

THE HUNT

Editor's Note: In the fall of 1968, Lon Winters and his brother-in-law, Bill Vogt, were elk hunting at Hannagans Meadow in Arizona. Deep in a canyon, Lon shot this great bull elk with a .308 Savage rifle. He and Bill had to quarter it and pack it out on Lon's best hunting horse, Pic. This story was written with the help and information obtained from the following people: Lon Winters, Bettie Jo Winters, Lanis Baker, Joe Mapes, Sharon Radonovich, and Bill Vogt.

Lon Winters was the epitome of an outdoor man. He was born 27 August 1917 in Globe, Arizona, the second child and only son of Crill and Ruby Winters (Ruby made the trip to the hospital on a donkey). At the time of his birth, the family was living in an area called Wheatfields, north of Globe, where Ruby's parents, Bill and

Cora Jackson, had a cattle ranch. Lon's dad worked as a cowboy on his father-in-law's and other local ranches. In 1921 Crill Winters homesteaded twenty acres about twelve miles northeast of Globe in an isolated area with no roads; the only access was by horseback. Crill and Ruby packed in lumber and furniture by mule to build and furnish their home. Shortly thereafter, Crill bought the forest-grazing permit from a man named Herb House, borrowed money from his employer and friend, John Griffen, and Winters Ranch was born.

Lon and his older sister, Stella, lived in their own little world of horses, cattle, dogs, and their parents. Their only contact with the outside world was an occasional visit from a relative or a cowboy from one of the big outfits. When a stranger did show up, Lon and Stella would head for the bushes and hide out like wild animals.

In about 1923 the family went over the mountain to Jackson's cattle ranch for Christmas, and when they returned home, they found their little ranch house burned to the ground. So again they had to pack in the lumber and furnishings for a house.

About this time, the family moved to Copper Hills, a community about five miles north of Globe, where Lon and Stella attended school and Crill rode horseback to and from the ranch whenever possible. In 1925 Lon's sister, Stella, developed severe asthma, and a doctor recommended a change in climate. In 1928 Ruby and the children moved to Phoenix. Crill would come from the ranch every two or three weeks to be with his family, then the whole family would spend the summer back at the ranch. By this time, they could access the ranch by going from Globe to San Carlos, then up Seven Mile Wash and on up to McMillanville, an old mining camp about fifty miles from Globe. From there they would walk about two miles up to the ranch house. Finally a makeshift road was completed to the house.

When Highway 60 came through, it changed the whole way of life for the Winters family. The Great Depression forced Ruby and the children to move back to the ranch. What had been a day's drive in dry weather to Globe was now about thirty minutes. By this time, Lon was a junior in high school. Never happy with town life, he quit school and went to work with his dad on the ranch.

The upper part of the ranch was very steep, rocky, and mountainous with deep thickets, and in those days the only cattle that could survive there were very wild, and had to be roped and led out of the hills in order to be sold. It took wild and fearless cowboys to get it done, and Lon was one of the best. He had good teachers, including his dad, his uncles, Riley and Joe Jackson, Lloyd McClain, Roland Jones, and others.

Lon's dad was a really good bronco rider and before coming to Globe had broken horses for a living for some of the big outfits. Like many young men, Lon wanted to be like his dad, so he and two of his buddies—one of whom was Chuck Shepherd, who became a world champion cowboy—took off for Wyoming, Idaho, and Montana to make a fortune riding broncos in summer rodeos. Lon soon found out he was no bronco rider and ended up sorting potatoes in Idaho. A letter to his dad brought enough money to get him back home.

When World War II came along, Lon went into the army in 1943 and spent the next three years in the Medical Corps. In the South Pacific he encountered several of his cowboy buddies. Rumor had it that the "powers that be" put former cowboys into the Medical Corps because they had worn cowboy boots so long they could not walk in GI shoes and therefore could not be foot soldiers.

When Lon returned home in 1946 after the war, he more or less took over running the ranch because of his father's poor health. He saw writing on the wall that said "No profit in wild cattle," so he started gathering the wild ones and replacing them with good gentle cattle. It was not an easy task, but he and his cowboy buddies loved it. Many stories were told about their efforts.

Lon married Betty Simpson in 1951, and they had three children, Lanis, Sharon, and Lonnie. To send the children to school, they moved from the ranch into Globe, with Lon commuting to the ranch.

Lon was an excellent trapper. As a young man and before the environmentalists took over and trapping became illegal, Lon ran two or three traplines during the winter. He caught coyotes, bobcats, foxes, badgers, and a few ring-tailed cats. The hides brought pretty good money then, and he did well working the ranch and trapping on the side. In later years Lon started

Lon Winters.

trapping again, but only for predators, mostly mountain lions.

In an area of the ranch called The Mountain, mountain lions saw to it that he had practically no calf crop in some years. At that time, when trapping was legal, he was paid a bounty for every lion scalp he sent in. During Lon's trapping days, he caught thirty-six lions and roped one out of a tree. In a rough area called Yankee Joe, there is a rather high, rocky bluff with a large laurel thicket. Lon would set in that one spot a trap under a low, drooping laurel limb, and over a few years he trapped thirteen lions.

While riding around and checking the cattle one early spring day, Lon heard his cow dogs barking and rode up to see what the ruckus was. They had a large mountain lion treed, but Lon did not have his gun with him. He couldn't ride off and leave that mountain lion alive, particularly since it was spring, and quite a few baby calves were on the ground. He got his rope, hung a loop on the end of a long pole, and made a snare. He then climbed up in the tree and snared the lion, jumped on his horse, and dragged the cat to its death. His sister, Bettie Jo, drove out to the ranch that evening and found Lon under a tree skinning the lion. He said, "Betcha can't find a bullet hole in this lion," and told his story.

"Lon," she said, "weren't you afraid when you were up in that tree with a mad lion?"

"Not at the time," he said, "but when I finally stopped my horse and knew the lion was dead, my hands were shaking so bad I couldn't roll a cigarette!"

Lon had only one true hobby, hunting. He and his brother-in-law, Bill Vogt, would head off with their horses and camp outfits to hunt elk, antelope, deer, wild turkey, and even javelina.

In the fall of 1968, Lon and Bill were elk hunting in Hannagans Meadow in Arizona when Lon dropped the huge bull elk deep in a canyon with his .308 Savage. He and Bill had to quarter it and pack it out on Lon's hunting horse, Pic.

In 1982 Lon and his sisters sold the ranch and Lon retired. He had an arthritic hip and couldn't spend long hours in the saddle. It was a difficult decision for all three of them—particularly Lon, who had spent a lifetime punching cows out there.

During his better days he was president of the Gila County Cattle Growers for two terms, served on a judging committee at the University of Arizona's Bull Sale, and was well known and respected for raising good-quality cattle.

Lon died 26 August 1994, the day before his seventy-seventh birthday. His relatives would love for him to know that he had bagged the "largest American elk in history." Maybe he does!

The following is what Lon's daughter and grandson wrote for his funeral:

Today we pay tribute to the memory of Alonzo Rex Winters, our grandfather and our hero. He was our very own John Wayne.... At the age of five Lon and his sister redeemed enough whiskey bottles to buy a saddle. Lon put the saddle on a burro and started his career at punching cattle. He represents the kind of bravery you just don't find anymore. We all loved the story of the treed mountain lion, and then there was the nests of rattlesnakes living under the house. The snakes had to go so they wouldn't get the dogs. Lon crawled under the house after the snakes. His religion in life was nature, the sunshine, the seasons, and most of all the rain.

Another fine comment came from Lon's friend Joe Mapes. When I told that Lon was being written about for killing this great bull elk, Joe said, "Lon deserves to be honored and written about without anything to do with the elk, just for being who he was—a friend, an honest man, and a great cowboy."

Alan Ellsworth holds the world-record typical rack he purchased from the Winters family.

Editor's note: In reading the accounts and my notes of what family and friends said and wrote about Alonzo Winters, I was reminded of how complimentary it is to be remembered as "a friend, an honest man." Taking the world-record elk was perhaps a reward for a good life.

The Discovery

Alan Ellsworth has been in the antler business since 1990, looking for sheds and buying, selling, and collecting large elk antlers. In 1995 Alan was pulling onto Main Street in Show Low, Arizona, when a truck drove past with an awesome elk rack in the back. When the driver pulled over at a local restaurant, Alan followed him into the parking lot to get a better look at the antlers. After some negotiating, Alan purchased the head. "I was fortunate enough to be in the right place at the right time," said Alan.

The rack was panel-measured at the Boone & Crockett Club's 23rd Big Game Awards in Reno, Nevada, in the spring of 1998. It was declared the new world record typical, surpassing the famous Plute bull by two-eighths of an inch.

The head photographed at the Rocky Mountain Elk Foundation convention.

NEW WORLD RECORD TYPICAL

Year: 1968

Location: White Mountains County, Arizona

Hunter: Alonzo Winters

Owner: Alan Ellsworth

	Typical Points				Nontypical Points	
	Right Antler	**Left Antler**	**Difference**		**Right Antler**	**Left Antler**
Main Beam Length	56 2/8	56 2/8	0	1st Point	0	2 1/8
1st Point	22 2/8	25 6/8	3 4/8	2nd Point		
2nd Point	29 0/8	25 6/8	3 2/8	3rd Point		
3rd Point	22 3/8	23 5/8	1 2/8	4th Point		
4th Point	24 5/8	22 0/8	2 5/8	5th Point		
5th Point	19 0/8	17 2/8	1 6/8	6th Point		
6th Point				7th Point		
7th Point				8th Point		
8th Point				9th Point		
1st Circumference	11 0/8	10 2/8	6/8	10th Point		
2nd Circumference	8 0/8	7 6/8	2/8	11th Point		
3rd Circumference	8 1/8	8 4/8	3/8	12th Point		
4th Circumference	6 5/8	7 7/8	1 2/8	13th Point		
				Subtotals	0	2 1/8
Total	207 2/8	205 0/8	15 0/8	Total	2 1/8	

DATA		TOTALS	
Number of Points Right	6	Inside Spread	47 4/8
Number of Points Left	7	Right Antler	207 2/8
Total Nontypical	2 1/8	Left Antler	205 0/8
Tip to Tip Spread	47 0/8	Typical Gross Score	459 6/8
Greatest Spread	52 0/8	Difference	-15 0/8
Inside Spread	47 4/8	Typical Net Score	444 6/8
		Nontypical	-2 1/8
Gross Score	459 6/8	Typical Score	442 5/8

FORMER WORLD RECORD
TYPICAL
PLUTE BULL

B&C 442 $^3/_8$

BY JIM ZUMBO

It was sometime around 1899 when John Plute looked down the iron sights of his .30-40 Krag and pulled the trigger. His shot was good, and he must have been overwhelmed at the size of the bull elk that lay dead from his bullet. Plute was an expert woodsman and skilled hunter with many elk to his credit, but this bull in Colorado's Dark Canyon was enormous. It was so big, in fact, that Plute was determined to pack the antlers out, something he had never done before. He hunted only for meat, but he wanted others to see this elk. No one would ever believe him otherwise.

More than half a century later, decades after Plute's death, the elk was officially declared the world record by the Boone & Crockett Club, scoring 442 $^3/_8$.

Unfortunately, no one attempted to document the details of the hunt back when Plute was alive. There was no Boone & Crockett Club in the early 1900s and therefore no standards by which to judge the elk. It was just a big bull, nothing special—until the measurement of its antlers some sixty years after Plute killed it. Much of the background information about the elk was theory, with various versions told and retold by writers and local residents who had no firsthand knowledge of it.

My investigation into the giant elk logically began with Ed Rozman, who owns the antlers. Rozman lives in Crested Butte, Colorado, an old mining town that underwent a profound transition after a ski area was built nearby several years ago. Two factions of humanity live in the lovely town ringed by massive mountain peaks—the longtime natives who followed railroads and worked the mines, and the new generation who live in condos, townhouses, and other modern homes.

Rozman belongs to the former. He was born and raised in the 8,888-foot-high valley that was settled by European immigrants, mainly Yugoslavians. This was also the place where John Plute lived, worked, and hunted.

I soon learned that no one knew when Plute was born or exactly when he died. Rozman and his wife, June, had unsuccessfully searched for Plute's grave in the Crested Butte cemetery. I couldn't find it, either, although the fact that Plute died in Crested Butte after being thrown from a horse is well documented.

Rudy Malensek, one of the few living people who knew Plute, gave this account of Plute's death.

Around 1922 there was a picnic at Malensek's ranch. Rudy was a teenager at the time, and remembers Plute taking off on a horse after having a few drinks. "John liked horses," Rudy said, "especially crazy ones. After he rode out and didn't return, I got worried about him. I went looking and found him piled up where the horse had thrown him. We took Plute to town and he died afterward."

Because Plute never married and had no family, few official records of him can be found. The mortuary in nearby Gunnison has no files prior to 1929. A check with Gunnison County turned up another John Plute, but he died when he was nineteen.

Finally, a persistent clerk found the death certificate of a John Pluth, who was born of Austrian parents in 1868 and died 10 October 1922. The cause of death was listed as a clot at the base of the brain that resulted from falling off a horse. This person was no doubt the John Plute that killed the elk, and Rozman believes that the name was misspelled on the certificate. Rozman's stepfather, John Rozich, ran a saloon in town, and Plute's name was evident in some of the bar ledgers that Rozman examined. According to the record, Plute would have been about thirty-one years old when he killed the elk, but even the 1899 date cannot be substantiated. He was fifty-four when he died.

Mary Sedmak, ninety-two, who lives in a Gunnison rest home, is the only person still alive who knew John Plute just after the turn of the century. Throughout the years, Mary has recounted details about Plute. She said he was a big, strong man who was basically a loner. He was quiet, loved to hunt, and, in fact, had hunted with Teddy Roosevelt when the former president visited the Colorado Rockies. Plute worked in the mines and headed for the mountains to hunt every chance he got.

Many folks say that Plute was a heavy drinker, but Mary and others who knew him said that he wasn't much different from anyone else in those days. Mining was a tough job. The men worked hard, and they all enjoyed leaning over saloon bars on their time off.

Plute lived alone in a boarding house, and it is said that he occasionally traded an elk quarter or two to pay for his room and board. He was no doubt looking for meat on the day he met up with the giant bull in Dark Canyon, which is twelve miles west of Crested Butte.

The precise history of the famous antlers is largely conjecture. A popular account is that after Plute killed the elk, he stored the rack in John Heuchemer's garage. (Rozman showed me a pitted spot on an antler that could have resulted from the rack lying on the dirt floor of the garage.) As the story continues, in 1915 Plute gave the rack to bar owner John Rozich in payment of a bar bill. Rozman told me that he carefully checked the bar's ledgers after he inherited the saloon from Rozich, his stepfather, and could find no record of the transaction. Mary Sedmak said that she remembered seeing the antlers on the barroom wall when she was very young, which indicates that the antlers were given to Rozich several years before 1915.

When John Rozich died in 1948, the Rozman brothers inherited the saloon along with the antlers, which up to that time amounted to nothing more than a conversation piece. In 1953 Ed Rozman took over the bar, and he soon realized that the rack might be special. A friend, Joe Wheeler, sent Rozman the 1952 edition of the Boone & Crockett record book in June 1954. Wheeler's brother-in-law was associated with the Boone & Crockett Club, and it was Wheeler's suggestion that Rozman have the elk scored.

In 1955 Ed and his brother, Tony, measured the rack. Working with no experience on a set of antlers that had enormous mass, the Rozmans gave it a score of 460. They sent the form to the Boone & Crockett Club in New York, but as a matter of procedure, Boone & Crockett officers couldn't accept the score and asked the Rozmans to have the rack officially measured.

Ed Rozman learned that there were two official measurers in Denver, but at that time he wasn't prepared to go to the expense of crating and shipping the rack. For the time being, the antlers continued to hang on the barroom wall.

Afterward, a member of the Hotchkiss Elks' Lodge stopped in the saloon to borrow a roulette wheel for one of the lodge's parties. The man looked at the giant antlers and asked if he could display them in the lodge. Ed Rozman agreed to loan the antlers if the lodge promised to have them officially measured. A deal was struck, and for the first time, the antlers left Crested Butte.

Three years later, Rozman attended a social function at the lodge and was disappointed to see the rack collecting dust in a back room atop an old phone booth. Club members said that they hadn't been able to find a van big enough to haul the rack to Denver, but they renewed their promise to have it officially scored.

The lodge contacted Jesse Williams, an official Boone & Crockett measurer who worked for the Colorado Division of Wildlife in Montrose.

"I was a little nervous when I walked into the lodge because I was in uniform," Williams told me. "The bartender was the only person in the bar and when I told him that I had been asked to measure the rack, he brought out a ladder. The rack was bolted very high up on the wall, and I almost lost my balance and dropped the antlers when I unbolted the skull and eased it away from the wall. I knew the rack was huge, but I absolutely couldn't believe my eyes when I finished measuring it. If my figures were right, this was the new world record! I measured it again, this time with much more care, and the second score was one-eighth-inch different from the first score."

When Williams's score sheet hit the Boone & Crockett Club in New York, officers were astonished. They immediately requested that the antlers be shipped to New York for final judging, and the lodge did so. In February 1962, John Plute's bull was formally recognized as the new world record elk.

Despite the discovery, Ed Rozman allowed the Elks' Lodge to display the rack for six more years. Throughout that period, the antlers remained only on the skull, as yet unmounted with a head and cape. In 1970 the Denver-based American Sportsman's Club told Rozman that they'd fit the elk on a shoulder mount if they could display it for a period in their home office. Rozman agreed, and the American Sportsman's Club turned the mounting job over to Denver taxidermist Joe Jonas.

The elk finally ended up in Crested Butte in 1971, and that's where it is today. I first saw the bull in February 1979, when I stopped in Crested Butte to ask of its whereabouts. After parking my truck next to fifteen-foot-high piles of snow on the street, I walked into a little hardware store to inquire about the antlers. I opened the door and gasped.

John Plute's elk wasn't being displayed in a prominent spot in a glamorous setting. It was in a 103-year-old store that, ironically, had been built about the time the world-record bull was born. As I gazed at the elk, a number of elderly men in bib coveralls huddled around the stove and rubbed their hands. A customer came in out of the −30 degree cold and bought a screwdriver from Tony Mihelich, owner of the store. Soon another man came in and asked

Tony if he could borrow a set of jumper cables to start his car. Tony grinned and walked out into the bitter cold to assist the stranger.

Tony, now eighty-two, is a pal of Ed Rozman's, and that's enough reason for the giant elk to hang in Tony's store. Ed asks nothing of Tony to display the bull, and Tony asks nothing of the thousands of people who come into the store every year to stare at the elk. Maybe Tony will sell a couple of flashlight batteries or a pair of pliers to someone, but more often than not, the people who stream into his place just want to look at the greatest bull in the world.

The lengths of the main beams are 55 $\frac{5}{8}$ and 59 $\frac{5}{8}$ inches; each of the first four points is more than twenty inches long. The right antler has eight points, the left seven. Despite the length and width of the antlers, what catches the eye quickest is their incredible mass. The circumference around each main beam between the first and second points, for example, is 12 $\frac{1}{8}$ and 11 $\frac{2}{8}$ inches; between the fourth and fifth points, the circumference is eight and nine inches.

The future of the world's biggest elk is in Ed Rozman's hands. Some collectors of record-class animals simply enjoy owning them while others deal in trophy antlers for profit. Rozman has neither goal. He never rents the elk out, as he could easily do, and now and then he'll let a buddy display the rack just for the heck of it. If you're in Gunnison for the annual Cattleman Days Festival in July, you'll probably see the elk in a local sporting-goods store, and you're apt to see it at the annual convention of the Rocky Mountain Elk Foundation. But after it's temporarily loaned out, it'll be back on the wall of Tony's hardware store in Crested Butte, between the cans of white gas and various nuts and bolts.

Rozman, at sixty-three, is about to retire as an employee of the water-treatment plant owned by a mining corporation just above town. He is moving to Paonia, Colorado, but the elk will stay in Tony's store.

As Rozman and I walked along the main street, chatting about the elk, I asked him what he intended to do with the bull.

"People have offered me as much as $50,000 for the elk," he told me, "but it's not for sale. I've been asked to give it to big museums where more people will see it in one day than will see it in a whole year here in Crested Butte, but I'm not interested."

I left town, driving past the little cemetery once more. It was a lovely day, with fleecy white clouds racing across a brilliant blue sky. Somewhere in that piece of ground, beneath the towering 12,049-foot Crested Butte peak, lie the forgotten remains of the man who killed the grandest bull ever known to civilization. It is a fitting place for John Plute to rest, and he would probably be pleased to know that his elk is just a few blocks down the road.

Editor's Note: Some years have passed since Jim wrote this story. Tony has passed away, and the bull now hangs in the Chamber of Commerce office in Crested Butte.

FORMER WORLD RECORD TYPICAL PLUTE BULL

Year: circa 1899
Hunter: John Plute

Location: Dark Canyon, Colorado
Owner: Ed Rozman

	Typical Points				Nontypical Points	
	Right Antler	Left Antler	Difference		Right Antler	Left Antler
Main Beam Length	55 5/8	59 5/8	4 0/8	1st Point	2 5/8	
1st Point	20 5/8	20 5/8	0	2nd Point		
2nd Point	27 3/8	25 5/8	1 6/8	3rd Point		
3rd Point	20 0/8	18 5/8	1 3/8	4th Point		
4th Point	22 4/8	21 5/8	7/8	5th Point		
5th Point	15 7/8	15 4/8	3/8	6th Point		
6th Point	11 7/8	7 3/8	4 4/8	7th Point		
7th Point				8th Point		
8th Point				9th Point		
1st Circumference	12 1/8	11 2/8	7/8	10th Point		
2nd Circumference	7 5/8	7 5/8	0	11th Point		
3rd Circumference	7 7/8	8 0/8	1/8	12th Point		
4th Circumference	8 0/8	9 0/8	1 0/8	13th Point		
				Subtotals	2 5/8	
Total	209 4/8	204 7/8	14 7/8	Total	2 5/8	

DATA		TOTALS	
Number of Points Right	8	Inside Spread	45 4/8
Number of Points Left	7	Right Antler	209 4/8
Total Nontypical	2 5/8	Left Antler	204 7/8
Tip to Tip Spread	39 6/8	Typical Gross Score	459 7/8
Greatest Spread	51 6/8	Difference	14 7/8
Inside Spread	45 4/8	Typical Net Score	445 0/8
		Nontypical	-2 5/8
Gross Score	457 2/8	Typical Score	442 3/8

CHAPTER 5

NUMBER 4 WORLD RECORD TYPICAL (UNOFFICIAL)

B&C 427 ³/8

This great elk, too, is part of the Meeker Hotel & Cafe collection. The hotel opened in 1896 and for more than 100 years has been a stopoff point for hunters, including such notables as Teddy Roosevelt. The hotel, which has been restored, has more than twenty-five mounts dating to the turn of the century. We can only guess how all the heads came to reside in the hotel. Perhaps back in the early 1900s, when people hunted mostly for meat, the antlers were given or sold to the hotel.

Sometime over the years this head fell off the wall, and four points have been repaired. Thus it cannot go into the record books at score of 427 ³/8. Officially, a point can be measured only up to a break.

A shot of the Meeker Hotel lobby in 1906. The bull is pictured on the left. The bear hide, bull in the background, and antler chair are there today. Photo courtesy Meeker Museum.

This old photo was a great find. Don Stemler and I found it in the archives of the Meeker Museum. As we travel the country we are always looking at old photos and trophies, trying to match them up and piecing together their history.

This photo shows the rack as I picked it up to be mounted. The old head was thrown away many years ago.

NUMBER 4 WORLD RECORD TYPICAL (UNOFFICIAL)

Year: Prior to 1906
Hunter: Unknown

Location: Meeker, Colorado area
Owner: Meeker Hotel & Cafe

	Typical Points				Nontypical Points	
	Right Antler	Left Antler	Difference		Right Antler	Left Antler
Main Beam Length	50 $^0/_8$	54 $^5/_8$	4 $^5/_8$	1st Point		
1st Point	19 $^0/_8$	19 $^6/_8$	$^6/_8$	2nd Point		
2nd Point	16 $^7/_8$	18 $^7/_8$	2 $^0/_8$	3rd Point		
3rd Point	19 $^1/_8$	18 $^0/_8$	1 $^1/_8$	4th Point		
4th Point	21 $^3/_8$	22 $^0/_8$	$^5/_8$	5th Point		
5th Point	22 $^7/_8$	21 $^1/_8$	1 $^6/_8$	6th Point		
6th Point	13 $^2/_8$	12 $^3/_8$	$^7/_8$	7th Point		
7th Point				8th Point		
8th Point				9th Point		
1st Circumference	11 $^5/_8$	11 $^3/_8$	$^2/_8$	10th Point		
2nd Circumference	12 $^6/_8$	9 $^2/_8$	3 $^4/_8$	11th Point		
3rd Circumference	8 $^0/_8$	8 $^6/_8$	$^6/_8$	12th Point		
4th Circumference	7 $^0/_8$	7 $^2/_8$	$^2/_8$	13th Point		
				Subtotals		
Total	201 $^7/_8$	203 $^3/_8$	16 $^4/_8$	Total		

DATA		TOTALS	
Number of Points Right	7	Inside Spread	38 $^5/_8$
Number of Points Left	7	Right Antler	201 $^7/_8$
Total Nontypical	None	Left Antler	203 $^3/_8$
Tip to Tip Spread	26 $^5/_8$	Typical Gross Score	443 $^7/_8$
Greatest Spread	47 $^2/_8$	Difference	-16 $^4/_8$
Inside Spread	38 $^5/_8$	Typical Net Score	427 $^3/_8$
		Nontypical	None
Gross Score	443 $^7/_8$	*Typical	427 $^3/_8$

*Points broken—cannot officially be entered.

MONTANA STATE RECORD
TYPICAL

B&C 419 ⁴/₈

HIGH, WIDE, AND HANDSOME
BY FRED C. MERCER

His track was big, but I never dreamed I was on the trail of the biggest rack ever shot in this century.

I woke up before daylight, aware that it was very cold in the tent. We were camped at an altitude of 9,200 feet on Cottonwood Creek in the Ruby River country of southwestern Montana. That's west of Yellowstone and a few miles north of the Idaho border. It was October 21, and by that season the nights in that high country are pretty sharp. The fire was out, so the cold wasn't surprising, but lying there, half awake, I thought the temperature had dropped since we'd crawled into our sacks the night before.

The ground under my sleeping bag felt lumpy and hard, and I decided against going back to sleep. I ran my eyes around the tent for a hint of gray light, but none showed. I unzipped my bag, found my flashlight, and shined it across to where Paul Stark's watch was hanging above his bedroll. Four o'clock; too early to get up. I lay back, zipped the bag shut, squirmed onto smoother ground, and dozed off again.

Nothing was farther from my mind than the idea that this might be my most exciting and satisfying day in twenty-three years of elk hunting.

Next thing I knew, I smelled smoke. That pulled me up, wide awake. I could hear voices. Some hunters camped near us were poking up their breakfast fire. Time for us to be stirring. Paul's watch said 4:15 now. I slid out of my bag, fumbled into my shirt, trousers, and pants, and untied the tent flaps.

The ground was white with two inches of soft, dry snow, and more was coming down. In the dim light of early morning, it half blotted out the timber across Cottonwood Creek. But the snow was also a break.

Tracking snow is just about the greatest boon a hunter can hope for. But there along the upper Ruby, we don't often get it as early as the third week of October. We'd been hunting on bare ground, and had found it lean

business. Now, I told myself, I'd kill the bull I wanted.

Paul and I had left home with Delbert Karlstrom on the morning of October 18, the day before elk season opened in that area. We drove the seventy miles to Cottonwood Creek in a Jeep and a truck, towing a horse trailer with Flikka, our combination saddle and pack mare. Paul is my uncle, forty-six years old, and owner of a dairy ranch a few miles south of Twin Bridges, Montana. I'm thirty-nine and work for him on the ranch. Delbert, his brother-in-law, is depot agent for the Northern Pacific at Logan, just east of Three Forks. The three of us have hunted together for years.

We camped on Cottonwood Creek the first time in 1946, and I'd been back there seven falls out of twelve since. This time we'd pitched our tent where the Burnt Creek road—a rough, unsurfaced Jeep and truck trail—crosses Cottonwood Creek, in the Gravely Range two miles east of the main Ruby River road and forty south of the town of Alder. It was the fall of 1958, and that area was open under regular license, for bull elk only. I was after something special, and I had a hunch from my previous trips that I'd find it in the rough and roadless country north of camp.

I started hunting elk in 1935, and a year later made my first kill—a cow in the Whitetail Range east of Butte.

In my book, the elk is the finest trophy animal in the West, and there's none I'd rather hunt.

I've been pretty successful at it too. Between 1935 and 1958, I had taken five six-point bulls (here in the West we count points on one side only; an Easterner would call our six-point elk twelve-pointers); I'd also taken five five-pointers, two spikehorns, and six cows. Now I figured it was time I hung up something better than just elk venison, although I'll admit that's hard to beat when it comes to good eating. I wanted a trophy head, something for the book. I love the mountains, and there's a challenge in tracking a bull elk through the rough going of his high-altitude haunts that I don't find in following any other game. But I certainly didn't expect to find the kind of elk I did.

Paul and Delbert and I made things snug for a week of hunting. We usually allow ourselves that much time. We started hunting on Monday, October 20, and worked hard that day without getting a shot. The snow came on Tuesday morning; the minute I saw it I figured it meant a change of luck.

I roused Delbert and Paul, walked the few steps to our cook tent, lit the gas lantern and one of our two gas stoves, broke ice on the water bucket, and put the coffee on. Then I started a fire in the barrel stove to warm things up.

Cottonwood Creek was brawling down its rocky channel, making a loud racket in the stillness of the morning. Over the noise of it I heard Flikka nicker, begging for a handout, and I walked down and poured her a ration of oats. Paul or Delbert would lead her to water while I cooked breakfast.

Flikka is a steady old gal, and we wouldn't dream of going elk hunting without her. She belongs to Paul's son, Bob. He's sixteen, and she is only a year younger.

I don't like to ride a horse while hunting, for several reasons. In timber, a horse puts me up among the low branches, where I can't see nearly so far or well. If there's snow on the trees, it brushes off on me. On foot, I can avoid it. I can walk quieter than any horse, and that's important in hunting either elk or mule deer. Finally, an elk will often go through timber too thick or up a slope too steep for a horse to carry a rider. I want to be able to follow, no matter where my elk goes, so I stay out of the saddle.

Delbert feels the same way. Paul doesn't; he likes to hunt from a horse, so he rides Flikka a fair share of the time.

But it's when we kill an elk in a spot we can't reach by Jeep (and there are plenty of 'em where we do our hunting) that Flikka comes in handy. That mare has paid her way many times, packing elk quarters out to the nearest Jeep road.

I went ahead with breakfast while Paul and Delbert doused their faces in ice water, watered Flikka, and fixed her up with hay.

We didn't hurry. Snow was still sifting down, and tracking conditions were getting better by the minute. Besides, more than once on such a morning, the three of us have knocked over an elk or muley within two hundred yards of camp. We figure it makes no sense to start out before full light and spook game when you can't see to shoot it.

By the time we finished breakfast there were three inches of snow on the ground. We made plans. I voted for a rough chunk of mountains east of Maverick Basin, across Geyser Creek and about a mile north of camp. I knew there were big bulls in there. It was a tough place to hunt—steep ridges, small creeks, canyons, and rocky peaks. But now that we had tracking snow, I figured my chances would be as good there as anywhere. In hunting elk, as with all game, you have to look for them where they are, and trophy bulls don't hang out in back yards. Delbert and Paul decided they'd hunt the same general area—Del on foot, Paul riding Flikka.

When our lunches were ready, I made up my pack. I tote an army pack sack that holds all the gear I need. I always take along extra gloves, a vacuum bottle of coffee, several candy bars, a flashlight, ten feet of quarter-inch rope, a hatchet, matches in a waterproof container, and a few stubs of candle for starting fires if I can't find dry wood. At one time or another, I've used every one of those items on a hunt, and was glad I had them.

The flashlight is one of the most important. I like to hunt late, especially if I'm on a good track. More than once I've taken elk because I stayed on a track until almost dark. Of course that means hiking to camp in pitch dark. It's not unusual for me to straggle in two or three hours after dark, and I've come in as late as midnight. In rough mountain country a flashlight is a must at such times. I've never had to stay out overnight, but it's probable I will one of these days. I go prepared for it, and it won't worry me. And my hunting partners know my methods well enough that it won't cause them any concern.

I don't carry a compass; I don't need one where I hunt. My father taught me when I was a youngster to find my way by keeping close watch of mountains, ridges, passes, canyons, streams, and other landmarks. That way, I won't get lost in our country. Once I know that darkness is going to overtake me before I get back to camp, I map out mentally the route I'll take, and carefully note every landmark I'll need to guide me in.

The pack I made up that morning on Cottonwood Creek weighed twelve or fifteen pounds, but it's not unusual for me to carry twenty-five to thirty. I dislike wearing a coat when hunting. I prefer to put on enough woolen shirts to keep me comfortable, and if there's wet snow on the brush, I carry a spare. Often I get warm and shed one; the pack comes in handy then, too.

When everything was ready, Paul shoved his rifle into the saddle boot and climbed onto Flikka. Del and I shouldered our packs and rifles (mine is a .270 Winchester Model 70), and trudged away from camp on foot. We took it slow and easy, keeping a sharp watch for elk or mule deer sign. We weren't too interested in muleys, for we had plenty of those nearer home, but if we got a crack at a trophy buck, we'd knock him over.

"If I find the track of a big elk today," I told my partners just as we started out, "I'm not coming back to camp until I kill him."

"What if it takes a week?" Paul kidded me.

"Then I'll stay out a week," I said. "But it won't take that long; I feel lucky."

Del and I crossed Geyser Creek, walked north another quarter of a mile, and split up. He turned east into thick timber, and I kept on north. I prefer to hunt by myself. One man makes less noise than two, and I'm free to go where I like and travel fast or slow. I see more game and have better luck when I'm alone. My two partners feel the same way, so nobody's feelings are hurt.

Farther on, I took to a steep, timbered draw that angled up the mountain to the northeast. Iron Creek ran down through it, there were steep ridges on either side, and the cover was heavy—a good place for elk to hole up. But before I'd gone far, I heard a noise behind me; Paul was riding up along the creek.

There was no sense in two of us working the same side of the street, so I turned to my left, panted up the steep slope, and broke out into fairly open timber on the crest of the ridge. I followed it for one hundred yards, and there found the snow scuffed up in a broad ribbon of elk tracks.

It was still snowing, but not as hard as at daylight, and sign was easy to read. There were at least nine or ten animals in the bunch; all but one left medium-size tracks. If hoofprints meant anything, I was following a big bull and his harem.

In studying the tracks, I decided I was on the trail of the biggest bull elk I'd ever run across. Overtaking him wouldn't be easy. The tracks indicated the elk were at least an hour ahead of me. It was now 7:30 A.M. They'd probably gone through here shortly after daybreak. In such weather they'd be likely to go down into heavy stuff and hole up for the day. The snow was soft but dry, and I'd have to use caution in tracking them.

What little wind there was came from the north. But in timber it would be unpredictable. The elk knew the area better than I did, and the going would be rugged. I resigned myself to a hard day. Maybe it would take more than one day, but it would be the kind of elk hunting I like best—trailing on new snow, and matching wits with a mountain-wise old bull that knows all the ropes. I was confident that when and if I finally came to the end of that big track, I'd be looking at a real trophy head.

The elk were headed down into the draw I'd just left, and at first I figured Paul would hit their tracks as he rode up, but it didn't work out that way. Iron Creek was frozen and Flikka didn't like to cross it, so Paul climbed out of the draw behind me and rode off to the northwest, along the edge of Maverick Basin. Delbert was hunting too far to the south and east to cross the elk tracks. I didn't know it at the time, but win, lose, or draw, I had the big bull to myself.

I took the tracks, walking as fast and quietly as I could, and keeping my eyes and ears peeled. The bull and his cows went down into the bottom of the draw, crossed Iron Creek, worked northeast for half a mile, and recrossed the creek, going north. So far they were traveling into the wind, and I figured I had nothing to worry about on that score, but I hadn't made enough allowance for the wariness and cunning of the old bull.

After about an hour of tracking, I heard a sudden clatter off to my right; downwind a bunch of heavy animals busted out of thick cover, running straight away from me. The timber was too thick for me to catch a glimpse of them, but I knew well enough what had happened. The bull had led them around in a circle, back to a place where the wind would tip them off about anybody following their track. I'd walked right into the trap. I could only hope they weren't badly spooked.

I stayed on the track, and it took me half an hour to follow their circle around. They had crossed Iron Creek for the third time and angled back southwest. When I got to the place where I'd jumped them, the tracks went out at a run, but luckily I hadn't come too close. They must have picked up only a whiff of man smell, for they weren't badly scared; they ran a short way and then settled back to a walk. I knew now they were only half an hour ahead of me.

Now the wind picked up, and the snow was falling harder, but I didn't mind. The harder it blew, the less it would eddy this way and that in the timber.

The elk made a big circle, traveling east, then south, and back to the west, until they weren't more than a mile from our camp on Cottonwood Creek. They crossed Iron Creek once more, and after that the tracks lined out north; I had a good hunch where they were headed. Off that way lay some of the roughest country I'd ever hunted—more creeks, high hills, big parks, passes, and open mountainsides with broken, timbered canyons and gulches. I knew I could trust the elk to keep out of open places.

For three more hours I stayed on the track. Then I left it and struck northeast, hoping to get ahead of them. Off there on the headwaters of Iron Creek stood a high, sparsely timbered peak between two open ridges. Up over both ridges ran well-used elk trails, and from the peak I could look down on both. The nearer pass would be within three hundred yards, the other not more than four hundred. That's long shooting, but not too long for a .270 scoped with a 4X Weaver. I had killed a fine bull in that very spot a year or two before. If I could get there before the elk did, I'd have a good chance of doing business again.

It was an hour's hike and a hard climb from where I left their tracks to the top of the peak. If they got across the pass ahead of me, I'd have made my climb for nothing. I discarded all caution and hurried, for I was downwind and too far away for them to hear any noise I made. I jumped a small herd of mule deer and crossed one fresh elk track that I judged had been made by a young bull, but I wasted no time on any of this.

It was an hour after noon when I sweated to the top of the peak. I found a place out of the wind where I could put my back against a tree and look down on both passes. Then I leaned my rifle across a log within easy reach, and broke out my lunch. I wolfed it down and drank half the coffee. When I saw no sign of the elk at the end of half an hour, I figured they weren't coming my way. My best chance was to get back on the track and stay with them.

I put three candy bars in my pocket to munch on as I walked. That left three, half the coffee, and a little spare lunch in my sack—enough to see me through the night if it had to. I traded my wet gloves for a dry pair, slid into my pack, picked up my rifle, and headed down off the ridge. I figured I knew about where I could cut the elk tracks, a mile or two to the southwest. I hit them even sooner than I expected; the big bull was still with his gals.

The tracks led north and east now, angling and twisting through the timber, across ravines and small draws, avoiding parks and passes, heading generally into the wind. I could afford to hurry if I kept an eagle eye ahead.

I soon decided the elk didn't know they were being followed. Though they kept on the move, they weren't pushing. My chances were beginning to look better.

Finally I saw something move in the timber ahead. In a second or two I made out the brown and black shape of an elk walking among the trees. I could see no horns, so I settled down on one knee and lifted the .270 carefully to my shoulder to bring the scope into play. Three elk walked past the cross hairs, one after another, but there was no sign of antlers.

In a minute or two they ambled out of sight. No more showed up, but I was sure that nearby lurked the others—including the big bull. The three had shown no sign of uneasiness, and I knew they hadn't discovered me. If I worked things right, I was close to the end now. I told myself that the trophy head was as good as hanging on my wall. Anybody who has hunted elk twenty-three years ought to know better.

I moved ahead, making no more commotion than a cat walking on a feather pillow, straining my eyes for any hint of movement. I reached a place where the elk had turned and crossed a ravine, and headed toward a fairly open park. Now, for the second time, I decided to quit the trail. I'd climb a ridge, get above and ahead of them. Then, if they went through the park, the bull was mine.

As I turned away from the tracks, I got a sharp reminder of how foolish it is to let your guard down for even a second on such a hunt. Out of the corner of my eye, I saw something move. There, seventy-five yards away, a four-point bull was legging it across an opening.

I didn't get a shot at him, and didn't even try. I knew the bull I'd tracked since morning was a bigger animal. This was almost certainly the lone elk whose track I had crossed a while back. I was afraid he might go barging headlong into the herd and spook them all, but he had his own reasons for not trying that.

I turned back and picked up his track to find out what had happened. He'd been standing in a thicket, watching me, and lit out as soon as I took a step. His tracks crossed those of the herd, but he made no attempt to join them. They kept to the timber; he took off across the open ridge. I figured that the bull I was after was so big and tough that the youngster knew better than to go near the harem. A bull elk in his prime tolerates no nonsense of that kind.

The herd couldn't be much more than five minutes ahead of me now, and I decided it would be best to follow them, after all. Shortly they turned up a steep mountainside, along the bottom of a rough canyon. The timber was mostly fir, not too dense but thick enough so that I could see no more than fifty to one hundred yards ahead.

It was hard climbing, for I was up around 10,000 feet and the air was thin. But I made the best time I could, knowing that when the elk reached the open ridge at the head of the canyon, they'd cross in a hurry and hit thicker timber on the far side. I had trailed the bunch twelve or fifteen miles now, and I was getting tired. I realized that unless I made my kill here on this ridge, I wasn't going to make it today.

I labored up the mountain for three-quarters of an hour, drenched with sweat, fighting for breath, pulling myself up the steepest places by hanging onto trees, and close to complete exhaustion. Then the slope began to level off, and I knew I was close to the top. Careful now! Somewhere on the ridge, or just

beyond, I'd get my chance—if I was going to get it at all.

The tracks turned left in single file and went down into a little timbered ravine. The open ridge lay just beyond. I mustered enough strength to run down the slope of the ravine and scramble up the other side. When I poked my head over the rim, the biggest bull elk I'd ever laid eyes on was standing broadside to me, not fifty yards away!

He was feeding, head down, but even in that position he was the most magnificent wild thing I had ever seen. His brown coat rippled over his bulky body with every move he made, his mane stood out black against the snowy mountainside, and his heavy-tined, white-tipped rack looked almost as tall as a man. Everything about him spoke of strength and arrogance; I didn't wonder that the younger bull had given him a wide berth.

There were other elk all over the place, but I didn't pay any attention to them. I sized up the big bull in a hurry, not wasting much time in admiration. This was the best shot I could hope for. If he discovered me, he'd reach the timber in three or four long strides.

I was breathing too hard for steady shooting, and maybe I had a touch of buck fever as well, for I'd never seen anything like this bull. But I had no choice.

The snow had stopped half an hour earlier. When I'm hunting in wet snow, I protect my scope with a cloth around the end, tucked in, not tied, so I'm ready for a quick shot, but I hadn't found that necessary this time. I'd checked the scope frequently all day, and the dry snow hadn't bothered it.

I put the cross hairs on the bull's heavy neck just behind the ears. Before I could squeeze the trigger, he seemed to sense danger; he threw up his head and looked off down the ridge.

I got on him again, picking the same spot, and slammed my 150-grain softpoint into him. I saw his whole body shake and knew I had done severe damage, but I didn't wait for him to go down. I bolted in a second hull and belted him again, in about the same place. He crumpled and fell like a dishrag.

From where I stood, I counted twelve cows in the open timber around him, all within one hundred feet. They milled for a minute, and some of them stood and stared at him, uncertain what had happened. Then a gaunt old

Fred Mercer with the big rack, October 1958.

girl lit out over the ridge, and the others broke and followed.

I fed two fresh shells into the Winchester .270 to replace the two I'd used, and walked carefully toward him. A wounded elk with a spark of life can be pure poison. My brother had a close call a few years back when he tried to cut the throat of a bull he had flattened. The elk wasn't quite finished, and he lunged, caught my brother, and pinned him down. If his hunting companion hadn't been near enough to hear him yell, he'd have been in bad trouble.

I didn't want anything like that to happen to me, and this fellow was nothing to fool with. But there was no need for caution. He was as dead as a smoked salmon. The first shot had hit in the neck six inches behind the head, about three inches low, grazing the windpipe. The second had shattered the spine just above the first.

I took five minutes to look him over and admire the head. He had seven points on each beam, a royal rack (it takes seven to qualify as a royal), the dream of every man who hunts elk, and the first I'd ever taken in that class. I'd done better than I'd dared hope. But I still didn't know just how much better.

I couldn't get enough of looking at him, but there was work to do, and I knew better than to lose time. I got the rope out of my pack, threw a loop over an antler, and worked him around until he was headed downhill. I guessed his weight at 1,200 pounds, far too heavy for one man to handle under ordinary conditions, but he skidded fairly well on the snow, and I managed to ease him down to an open spot where I would dress him out.

Dressing an animal of that size is a bigger chore than you think until you've tried it. My knife was sharp and I worked fast, but it took me well over half an hour. When I finished, I had only about an hour of daylight left. I was seven miles from camp as an eagle would travel, and a lot farther the way I'd have to go. We drove twenty-one miles with the Jeep getting back to the elk the next day.

I ate all my candy bars, finished my coffee, pulled the last pair of dry gloves from the pack, took a careful look at the landmarks on all sides so I'd have no trouble finding my way back to the kill in the morning, and trudged off down the ridge.

It was a long hike for a tired man, but I knew the country and was back at camp a couple of hours after full dark. It snowed most of the way. There were five inches on the ground when I got in, and two more the next morning.

Fortunately I had killed the elk in about the only spot for miles around that we could reach by Jeep. As a result, Flikka missed a tough assignment. We drove in along the ridge, and getting the head and quarters back to camp proved easier than we expected.

I realized I had taken an exceptional head, and when we got home I borrowed the Boone & Crockett Club book, *Records of North American Big Game*, from Frank Rose's Sport Shop at Twin Bridges. Following the book's instructions, I put a tape on the horns; the results must have made my eyes pop. Unless I was making a mistake, I'd taken one of the really good elk heads of all time.

I lost no time getting in touch with Joe Gaab, a Montana conservation officer at Livingston, who's also an official measurer for Boone & Crockett. He confirmed my opinion, and even went me a couple of points better.

The outstanding thing about the head was the length of the horns: a fraction over 59 inches, less than an inch short of five feet. The inside spread of the main beams was 53 inches, the greatest outside spread 56. Gaab's official score gave my trophy 419 4/8 points, and this has since been confirmed by the Boone & Crockett Club in New York.

I had killed the best elk ever taken in Montana, and the second best on record anywhere, bettering the No. 2 head on the Boone & Crockett list, which was taken on the Wieser River in Idaho in 1954. That bull scored 414 4/8 points. The world-record head, scoring a whopping 441 6/8, was taken in the Big Horn Mountains of Wyoming back in 1890. Winter range for elk was better in those days, and the bulls grew bigger racks. Boone & Crockett Club officials predict that's a record likely to stand for years to come. That's all right with me. I'm satisfied with No. 2 spot.

Editor's Note: Fred Mercer passed away in 1999. His story ran in the January 1960 issue of Outdoor Life *magazine. It is reprinted here courtesy of Mrs. Mercer.*

MONTANA STATE RECORD
TYPICAL

Year: 1958
Hunter: Fred C. Mercer

Location: Madison County, Montana
Owner: Rocky Mountain Elk Foundation

	Typical Points				Nontypical Points	
	Right Antler	Left Antler	Difference		Right Antler	Left Antler
Main Beam Length	59 7/8	60 1/8	2/8	1st Point		
1st Point	17 6/8	17 2/8	4/8	2nd Point		
2nd Point	16 3/8	15 5/8	6/8	3rd Point		
3rd Point	16 4/8	16 6/8	2/8	4th Point		
4th Point	23 7/8	22 3/8	1 4/8	5th Point		
5th Point	18 3/8	19 7/8	1 4/8	6th Point		
6th Point	4 0/8	4 2/8	2/8	7th Point		
7th Point				8th Point		
8th Point				9th Point		
1st Circumference	9 2/8	9 3/8	1/8	10th Point		
2nd Circumference	7 1/8	7 2/8	1/8	11th Point		
3rd Circumference	7 1/8	6 7/8	2/8	12th Point		
4th Circumference	6 1/8	6 0/8	1/8	13th Point		
				Subtotals		
Total	186 3/8	185 6/8	5 5/8	Total		

DATA		TOTALS	
Number of Points Right	7	Inside Spread	53 0/8
Number of Points Left	7	Right Antler	186 3/8
Total Nontypical	None	Left Antler	185 6/8
Tip to Tip Spread	48 2/8	Typical Gross Score	425 1/8
Greatest Spread	55 3/8	Difference	-5 5/8
Inside Spread	53 0/8	Typical Net Score	419 4/8
		Nontypical	None
Gross Score	425 1/8	Typical Score	419 4/8

43

CHAPTER 7

OREGON STATE RECORD TYPICAL

B&C 418 $^0/_8$

AS TOLD TO THE AUTHOR BY JOE AND PAULA JESSEL

On a cool November afternoon in 1942, Opal Evans was in camp preparing for the evening meal when she heard a crashing through the brush behind her. Looking up, Opal saw a huge bull elk approaching the camp. It so frightened her that she ran and jumped into the pickup and locked the doors. She still recalls how funny it was that she locked the doors when telling the story to her grandson, Joe Jessel.

Later in the day, when her husband, Hugh, returned to camp along with Opal's brother, Leonard Ferguson, Opal told the men about the elk. She said it was a large bull with a gray beard and a huge set of antlers. The next morning the men went out on their hunt, and about 10 A.M. Hugh shot a bull with his .300

Savage. When they returned to camp with the elk, Opal said that it was the same bull she had seen the day before.

The hunters didn't realize the trophy they had, and the antlers were tossed from barn to barn for the next thirty-five years. Then, in 1977, they were hung in an oak tree at the home of the Evans's daughter, JoAnne Jessel, and put to use as a flowerpot hanger.

This was the tale told to Joe during research into the background of a bull elk shot by his grandfather, Hugh Evans, near Mitchell in the Ochoco National Forest in central Oregon in 1942.

In 1991 Joe was on vacation visiting a taxidermist friend, Rich Eckert. Joe asked Rich if he could restore an old set of antlers that were hanging in an oak tree in his mother's yard. Rich said he could restore them and mount them on a head. Soon after, Joe's wife, Paula, and his mother-in-law, Pat, strapped the antlers on top of Pat's Toyota Camry and traveled across the state of Oregon to pass the antlers on to the taxidermist. On the way, Pat was pulled over and cited for speeding. However, both women felt the officer pulled them over to get a closer look at the rack.

After the restoration was complete, Eckert told them that they probably had a record elk on their hands and that they should get someone from Boone & Crockett to score it. Joe tried in vain for over a year to get an official out to their home in Molalla to score the mount.

Finally, he took the mounted rack to the Sportsmen Show in Portland, where it was scored unofficially at 419 3/8.

The mount went back to the couple's home and later into a local museum. When the museum closed, the mount was on display at a local auto-parts store.

In September of 1994, Gary Wise, owner of the store, was finally able to get Charles (Rusty) Linberg, an official scorer for Boone & Crockett, to come out to the store and score the antlers officially at 418, making it the largest on record in the state of Oregon. This should also place it in the top ten in the world for Boone & Crockett.

Hunter Hugh Evans, sitting, and his brother-in-law, Leonard Ferguson, kneeling, with the Oregon record bull and a 1935 Chevy pickup truck.

OREGON STATE RECORD
TYPICAL

Year: 1942
Hunter: Hugh Evans

Location: Crook County, Oregon
Owner: Joe Jessel

	Typical Points				Nontypical Points	
	Right Antler	Left Antler	Difference		Right Antler	Left Antler
Main Beam Length	63 2/8	64 2/8	1 0/8	1st Point		
1st Point	18 5/8	18 7/8	2/8	2nd Point		
2nd Point	20 2/8	19 1/8	1 1/8	3rd Point		
3rd Point	19 1/8	18 1/8	1 0/8	4th Point		
4th Point	19 5/8	22 3/8	2 6/8	5th Point		
5th Point	13 5/8	12 6/8	7/8	6th Point		
6th Point	5 7/8	7 2/8	1 3/8	7th Point		
7th Point				8th Point		
8th Point				9th Point		
1st Circumference	10 1/8	9 6/8	3/8	10th Point		
2nd Circumference	8 1/8	7 6/8	3/8	11th Point		
3rd Circumference	7 4/8	7 4/8	0	12th Point		
4th Circumference	7 4/8	7 7/8	3/8	13th Point		
				Subtotals		
Total	193 5/8	195 5/8	9 4/8	Total		

DATA			TOTALS	
Number of Points Right	7		Inside Spread	38 2/8
Number of Points Left	7		Right Antler	193 5/8
Total Nontypical	None		Left Antler	195 5/8
Tip to Tip Spread	25 1/8		Typical Gross Score	427 4/8
Greatest Spread	49 7/8		Difference	-9 4/8
Inside Spread	38 2/8		Typical Net Score	418 0/8
			Nontypical	None
Gross Score	427 4/8		Typical Score	418 0/8

CHAPTER 8

WASHINGTON STATE RECORD
TYPICAL
SHEDS

B&C 413 $^2/_8$

Wilson Gulick was riding along a trail on a pack trip in the summer of 1925 when he spotted a large elk shed. He passed it and proceeded on down the trail. But after thinking about how big it looked, he returned, picked it up, and put it on his packhorse.

On down the trail lay the other side of the shed. The pair has been in his family for seventy-five years.

Mike Rodgers, owner of Painted Rock Outfitters, acquired them from Wilson's son, Monte Holmes, to display in his lodge in Darby, Montana.

Mike Rodgers holding the sheds.

WASHINGTON STATE RECORD TYPICAL SHEDS

Year: 1925 **Location: Kittitas County, Washington**
Hunter: Wilson Gulick & Monte Holmes Owner: Mike Rodgers

	Typical Points				Nontypical Points	
	Right Antler	Left Antler	Difference		Right Antler	Left Antler
Main Beam Length	63 3/8	64 3/8	1 0/8	1st Point		
1st Point	18 3/8	18 7/8	4/8	2nd Point		
2nd Point	16 6/8	16 4/8	2/8	3rd Point		
3rd Point	13 0/8	12 4/8	4/8	4th Point		
4th Point	23 6/8	25 3/8	1 5/8	5th Point		
5th Point	19 3/8	16 2/8	3 1/8	6th Point		
6th Point	7 3/8	0	7 3/8	7th Point		
7th Point				8th Point		
8th Point				9th Point		
1st Circumference	9 3/8	9 4/8	1/8	10th Point		
2nd Circumference	7 6/8	7 6/8	0	11th Point		
3rd Circumference	9 2/8	8 4/8	6/8	12th Point		
4th Circumference	9 1/8	8 6/8	3/8	13th Point		
				Subtotals		
Total	197 4/8	188 3/8	15 5/8	Total		

DATA		TOTALS	
Number of Points Right	7	Inside Spread	43 0/8
Number of Points Left	6	Right Antler	197 4/8
Total Nontypical	None	Left Antler	188 3/8
Tip to Tip Spread	27 3/8	Typical Gross Score	428 7/8
Greatest Spread	47 0/8	Difference	-15 5/8
Inside Spread, Estimated	43 0/8	Typical Net Score	413 2/8
		Nontypical	None
Gross Score	428 7/8	Typical Score	413 2/8

CHAPTER 9

NUMBER 2 MONTANA STATE RECORD TYPICAL

B&C 404 ⁶/₈

Carl Snyder first spotted the wide-racked bull at 1,000 yards. The chase was on. Over a three-day period he spotted and tracked the bull numerous times but could not get close enough for a shot.

He was ready to give up when the bull finally stepped out in the open. It was a long shot but a good one. Carl's trophy of a lifetime had covered twenty-five miles.

NUMBER 2 MONTANA STATE RECORD TYPICAL

Year: 1959
Hunter: Carl Snyder

Location: Mineral County, Montana
Owner: Warren and Rick Stone

	Typical Points				Nontypical Points	
	Right Antler	Left Antler	Difference		Right Antler	Left Antler
Main Beam Length	58 6/8	57 0/8	1 6/8	1st Point		
1st Point	16 7/8	17 0/8	1/8	2nd Point		
2nd Point	17 4/8	16 5/8	7/8	3rd Point		
3rd Point	18 7/8	21 1/8	2 2/8	4th Point		
4th Point	21 4/8	22 2/8	6/8	5th Point		
5th Point	15 1/8	15 0/8	1/8	6th Point		
6th Point	3 7/8	5 3/8	1 4/8	7th Point		
7th Point	1 2/8	0	1 2/8	8th Point		
8th Point				9th Point		
1st Circumference	9 5/8	9 1/8	4/8	10th Point		
2nd Circumference	6 6/8	7 0/8	2/8	11th Point		
3rd Circumference	6 4/8	6 4/8	0	12th Point		
4th Circumference	6 7/8	6 5/8	2/8	13th Point		
				Subtotals		
Total	183 4/8	183 5/8	9 5/8	Total		

DATA		TOTALS	
Number of Points Right	8	Inside Spread	47 2/8
Number of Points Left	7	Right Antler	183 4/8
Total Nontypical	None	Left Antler	183 5/8
Tip to Tip Spread	34 3/8	Typical Gross Score	414 3/8
Greatest Spread	54 0/8	Difference	-9 5/8
Inside Spread	47 2/8	Typical Net Score	404 6/8
		Nontypical	None
Gross Score	414 3/8	Typical Score	404 6/8

CHAPTER 10

NUMBER 2 COLORADO STATE RECORD TYPICAL SHEDS

B&C 400 $^3/_8$

Guy Stealey found this great set of sheds in 1936 on the Pothole Ranch east of Buford, Colorado.

In 1940 Guy gave the sheds to Ken Dunbar, the local taxidermist in Meeker, Colorado, to put on display. They remain in the Dunbar family today. Keith Dunbar made arrangements to display the head in the Meeker Hotel after the 1999 World Record Elk Tour was completed.

The antlers before they were restored.

NUMBER 2 COLORADO STATE RECORD TYPICAL SHEDS

Year: 1936
Hunter: Guy Stealey

Location: Rio Blanco County, Colorado
Owner: Keith Dunbar

	Typical Points				Nontypical Points	
	Right Antler	Left Antler	Difference		Right Antler	Left Antler
Main Beam Length	56 6/8	55 3/8	7/8	1st Point		
1st Point	19 2/8	19 3/8	1/8	2nd Point		
2nd Point	21 6/8	17 7/8	3 7/8	3rd Point		
3rd Point	19 3/8	22 4/8	3 1/8	4th Point		
4th Point	21 3/8	22 1/8	6/8	5th Point		
5th Point	13 0/8	14 0/8	1 0/8	6th Point		
6th Point				7th Point		
7th Point				8th Point		
8th Point				9th Point		
1st Circumference	8 1/8	8 4/8	3/8	10th Point		
2nd Circumference	6 6/8	7 1/8	3/8	11th Point		
3rd Circumference	7 6/8	7 7/8	1/8	12th Point		
4th Circumference	8 2/8	8 2/8	0	13th Point		
				Subtotals		
Total	182 4/8	183 4/8	10 5/8	Total		

DATA		TOTALS	
Number of Points Right	6	Inside Spread	45 0/8
Number of Points Left	6	Right Antler	182 4/8
Total Nontypical	None	Left Antler	183 4/8
Tip to Tip Spread	Unknown	Typical Gross Score	411 0/8
Greatest Spread	48 5/8	Difference	-10 5/8
Inside Spread, Estimated	45 0/8	Typical Net Score	400 3/8
		Nontypical	None
Gross Score	411 0/0	Typical Score	400 3/8

CHAPTER 11

WORLD RECORD
NONTYPICAL
SHEDS

B&C 475 $^2/_8$

This great set of sheds was picked up in Colorado in the late 1800s or early 1900s by William Wood, the great-great-grandfather of Julia Troy. The antlers were bolted to a board and hung in a farmhouse in Ohio for some eighty-five years. As a small child, Julia found the antlers intriguing. After Julia's grandfather passed away in 1985 and her grandmother in 1987, the antlers were passed on to her.

Fortunately, Julia took the antlers home—her grandparents' home was destroyed by fire in 1992.

Julia's brother and sister-in-law, Rex and Terri Summerfield, Idahoans who are avid elk hunters and Rocky Mountain Elk Foundation members, saw the antlers in the garage while visiting. They excitedly measured the antlers and took photos to send me. They felt the rack would rank high and be of great interest in the Eastmans' World Record Elk Tour.

The family is trying to uncover more information about the location and history on these great sheds.

Rex Summerfield holding the sheds. This was the photo he mailed to me with his story.

Todd and Julia Troy hold the huge shed antlers.

WORLD RECORD NONTYPICAL SHEDS

Year: Turn of the Century (1900) **Location:** Colorado
Hunter: William Wood **Owner:** Todd and Julia Troy

	Typical Points				Nontypical Points	
	Right Antler	Left Antler	Difference		Right Antler	Left Antler
Main Beam Length	60 $^7/_8$	54 $^2/_8$	6 $^5/_8$	1st Point	20 $^5/_8$	20 $^0/_8$
1st Point	18 $^2/_8$	17 $^4/_8$	$^6/_8$	2nd Point		2 $^1/_8$
2nd Point	20 $^2/_8$	20 $^5/_8$	$^3/_8$	3rd Point		2 $^5/_8$
3rd Point	16 $^4/_8$	16 $^5/_8$	$^1/_8$	4th Point		4 $^2/_8$
4th Point	20 $^5/_8$	21 $^0/_8$	$^3/_8$	5th Point		
5th Point	20 $^4/_8$	18 $^1/_8$	2 $^3/_8$	6th Point		
6th Point	12 $^1/_8$	6 $^1/_8$	6 $^0/_8$	7th Point		
7th Point				8th Point		
8th Point				9th Point		
1st Circumference	10 $^0/_8$	9 $^4/_8$	$^4/_8$	10th Point		
2nd Circumference	8 $^2/_8$	7 $^3/_8$	$^7/_8$	11th Point		
3rd Circumference	10 $^6/_8$	8 $^0/_8$	2 $^6/_8$	12th Point		
4th Circumference	9 $^2/_8$	8 $^7/_8$	$^3/_8$	13th Point		
				Subtotals	20 $^5/_8$	30 $^0/_8$
Total	207 $^3/_8$	188 $^0/_8$	20 $^7/_8$	Total	50 $^5/_8$	

DATA		TOTALS	
Number of Points Right	8	Inside Spread	50 $^6/_8$
Number of Points Left	12	Right Antler	207 $^3/_8$
Total Nontypical	50 $^5/_8$	Left Antler	188 $^0/_8$
Tip to Tip Spread	44 $^6/_8$	Typical Gross Score	446 $^1/_8$
Greatest Spread	67 $^0/_8$	Difference	-20 $^7/_8$
Inside Spread, Estimated	50 $^6/_8$	Typical Net Score	424 $^5/_8$
		Nontypical	+50 $^5/_8$
Gross Score	496 $^1/_8$	Nontypical Net Score	475 $^2/_8$

CHAPTER 12

NEW WORLD RECORD
NONTYPICAL
ARROWHEAD BULL

B&C 465 ²/₈

This great elk was found dead near Shelter Bay Ferry Landing on the upper Arrow Lakes on July 30, 1994. The Arrow Lakes are a 100-plus-mile stretch of the Columbia River beginning just north of the U.S. border and extending to Revelstoke, British Columbia. Shelter Bay is near the north end of the lakes.

The bull is believed to have lived near the old community of Arrowhead and is thus named the Arrowhead Bull. Stories are told of how other animals tried to swim the bay and end up dying in their efforts or are chased to shore by fishermen. This bull may have met the same fate as it tried to cross the bay and was slowed down by its huge antlers in velvet, struggling to keep its head above water.

Arrowhead Bull, photographed at the Boone & Crockett Club's 23rd Big Game Awards Program in 1998, where it was declared the new world record.

Roger Selner holds the world-record Arrowhead Bull after it was picked up in Canada to be mounted and taken on tour.

NEW WORLD RECORD NONTYPICAL ARROWHEAD BULL

Year: 1994

Found by: Animal found dead

Location: Shelter Bay on Upper Arrow Lakes, British Columbia, Canada

Owner: British Columbia Ministry of Environment

	Typical Points				Nontypical Points		
	Right Antler	Left Antler	Difference			Right Antler	Left Antler
Main Beam Length	49 $^2/_8$	46 $^3/_8$	2 $^7/_8$	1st Point		15 $^0/_8$	11 $^1/_8$
1st Point	26 $^1/_8$	25 $^5/_8$	$^4/_8$	2nd Point		4 $^6/_8$	9 $^6/_8$
2nd Point	23 $^0/_8$	23 $^4/_8$	$^4/_8$	3rd Point		4 $^0/_8$	3 $^6/_8$
3rd Point	22 $^0/_8$	22 $^1/_8$	$^1/_8$	4th Point			1 $^4/_8$
4th Point	20 $^2/_8$	17 $^6/_8$	2 $^4/_8$	5th Point			5 $^1/_8$
5th Point	14 $^2/_8$	10 $^6/_8$	3 $^4/_8$	6th Point			
6th Point				7th Point			
7th Point				8th Point			
8th Point				9th Point			
1st Circumference	8 $^5/_8$	8 $^6/_8$	$^1/_8$	10th Point			
2nd Circumference	7 $^2/_8$	7 $^2/_8$	0	11th Point			
3rd Circumference	9 $^3/_8$	9 $^2/_8$	$^1/_8$	12th Point			
4th Circumference	9 $^7/_8$	13 $^6/_8$	3 $^7/_8$	13th Point			
				Subtotals		23 $^6/_8$	31 $^2/_8$
Total	190 $^0/_8$	185 $^1/_8$	14 $^1/_8$	Total		55 $^0/_8$	

DATA		TOTALS	
Number of Points Right	9	Inside Spread	49 $^2/_8$
Number of Points Left	11	Right Antler	190 $^0/_8$
Total Nontypical	55 $^0/_8$	Left Antler	185 $^1/_8$
Tip to Tip Spread	50 $^5/_8$	Typical Gross Score	424 $^3/_8$
Greatest Spread	61 $^0/_8$	Difference	-14 $^1/_8$
Inside Spread	49 $^2/_8$	Typical Net Score	410 $^2/_8$
		Nontypical	+55 $^0/_8$
Gross Score	479 $^3/_8$	Nontypical Net Score	465 $^2/_8$

CHAPTER 13

MANITOBA RECORD NONTYPICAL

B&C 455 ⁵/₈

Sean Burdeniuk was in search of a large elk to help feed his family. Under the Manitoba Tribal Treaty, he was permitted to take an elk for subsistence. At the time, the large set of antlers on the bull he shot had little importance to him; he knew the bull was well over a thousand pounds and would provide a lot of meat.

After he brought the bull home, everyone who saw the large set of antlers was just in awe. The bull was taken at the end of July while the antlers were still in velvet. The rack was stripped, dried, and recolored for mounting.

An outfitter friend, Randy Bean, heard about the big rack and, being a knowledgeable measurer, rough measured the antlers in the upper 450s. Randy called me with the information and felt that it would be a great elk for the tour. The bull scores high in Boone & Crockett and is in contention for the second largest nontypical elk.

Jeff Hints holds the rack after it was stripped of velvet before being recolored and mounted.

Sean Burdeniuk with his antlers just after the taking in July 1998.

MANITOBA RECORD NONTYPICAL

Year: 1998
Hunter: Sean Burdeniuk

Location: Ethelbert, Manitoba, Canada
Owner: Sean Burdeniuk

	Typical Points				Nontypical Points	
	Right Antler	Left Antler	Difference		Right Antler	Left Antler
Main Beam Length	48 ³/₈	49 ⁴/₈	1 ¹/₈	1st Point	20 ¹/₈	8 ⁵/₈
1st Point	19 ¹/₈	19 ⁰/₈	¹/₈	2nd Point	9 ²/₈	7 ²/₈
2nd Point	18 ⁵/₈	22 ⁰/₈	3 ³/₈	3rd Point		
3rd Point	24 ⁷/₈	20 ⁴/₈	4 ³/₈	4th Point		
4th Point	20 ⁷/₈	19 ⁷/₈	1 ⁰/₈	5th Point		
5th Point	15 ¹/₈	14 ⁰/₈	1 ¹/₈	6th Point		
6th Point	7 ⁰/₈	9 ⁵/₈	2 ⁵/₈	7th Point		
7th Point				8th Point		
8th Point				9th Point		
1st Circumference	11 ⁶/₈	12 ²/₈	⁴/₈	10th Point		
2nd Circumference	7 ⁷/₈	8 ⁰/₈	¹/₈	11th Point		
3rd Circumference	8 ³/₈	8 ⁰/₈	³/₈	12th Point		
4th Circumference	9 ²/₈	11 ⁰/₈	1 ⁶/₈	13th Point		
				Subtotals	29 ³/₈	15 ⁷/₈
Total	191 ²/₈	193 ⁶/₈	16 ⁴/₈	Total	45 ²/₈	

DATA		TOTALS	
Number of Points Right	9	Inside Spread	41 ⁷/₈
Number of Points Left	9	Right Antler	191 ²/₈
Total Nontypical	45 ²/₈	Left Antler	193 ⁶/₈
Tip to Tip Spread	44 ¹/₈	Typical Gross Score	426 ⁷/₈
Greatest Spread	56 ⁰/₈	Difference	-16 ⁴/₈
Inside Spread	41 ⁷/₈	Typical Net Score	410 ³/₈
		Nontypical	+45 ²/₈
Gross Score	472 ¹/₈	*Nontypical Score	455 ⁵/₈

Score pending on verification from awards program in summer, 2001.

CHAPTER 14

NUMBER 2 WORLD RECORD NONTYPICAL

B&C 449 ⁷/₈

Kevin Fugere, a rancher from Belfield, North Dakota, shot the elk of a lifetime on 15 August 1997. Not only does it exceed the minimum requirements for listing in the Boone & Crockett record book—385 inches for a nontypical elk—it exceeds the old world record by 2 ⁶/₈ inches and is the largest elk ever taken by a hunter.

Forty-seven elk were reintroduced into North Dakota's Theodore Roosevelt National Memorial Park in 1985. The animals came from the Wind Canyon National Park in South Dakota. Many of those elk have since escaped from the park and established herds outside the area.

After area ranchers and farmers complained about crop destruction and fence damage, forty-seven elk-hunting permits were issued—thirty to North Dakota residents in a lottery and seventeen to landowners adjacent to the park.

Kevin had previously hunted Montana and Wyoming for elk, taking a nice bull in Wyoming. He said the rack of his mounted bull from Wyoming fits inside the big bull's rack.

"I had heard of this big eight-point bull," Kevin said. "Thursday before the hunt I went out on horseback and rode until I found him."

Kevin, along with his brother, Blane, were out again on opening day. "I took Blane with me because things click when we hunt together," Kevin said. "He's a good hunter."

The brothers waited for the 11 A.M. opening and rode to where they watched the big bull bed down. Three shots from Kevin's 7mm Magnum resulted in a new North Dakota record and the No. 2 world record.

Don Stemler and I have looked at thousands of photos and hunted elk for many years. This bull has the largest body of any elk we have ever seen. Kevin, being a cattle rancher, guessed the bull's weight at between 1,100 and 1,200 pounds. We believe him.

Kevin, wife Cindy, and son Ian on the ranch in North Dakota, before the rack was picked up to mount for the tour.

The bull's weight was estimated at 1,100 pounds.

NUMBER 2 WORLD RECORD NONTYPICAL

Year: 1997
Hunter: Kevin Fugere

Location: Billings County, North Dakota
Owner: Kevin Fugere

	Typical Points				Nontypical Points	
	Right Antler	Left Antler	Difference		Right Antler	Left Antler
Main Beam Length	55 1/8	53 7/8	1 2/8	1st Point	10 2/8	7 5/8
1st Point	19 4/8	20 0/8	4/8	2nd Point	19 0/8	
2nd Point	16 1/8	17 2/8	1 1/8	3rd Point		
3rd Point	23 6/8	23 7/8	1/8	4th Point		
4th Point	21 1/8	19 7/8	1 2/8	5th Point		
5th Point	20 0/8	18 6/8	1 2/8	6th Point		
6th Point				7th Point		
7th Point				8th Point		
8th Point				9th Point		
1st Circumference	8 7/8	9 4/8	5/8	10th Point		
2nd Circumference	7 6/8	7 6/8	0	11th Point		
3rd Circumference	7 6/8	7 3/8	3/8	12th Point		
4th Circumference	8 3/8	9 2/8	7/8	13th Point		
				Subtotals	29 6/8	7 5/8
Total	188 3/8	187 4/8	7 3/8	Total	37 3/8	

DATA		TOTALS	
Number of Points Right	8	Inside Spread	44 0/8
Number of Points Left	7	Right Antler	188 3/8
Total Nontypical	37 3/8	Left Antler	187 4/8
Tip to Tip Spread	49 7/8	Typical Gross Score	419 7/8
Greatest Spread	58 2/8	Difference	-7 3/8
Inside Spread	44 0/8	Typical Net Score	412 4/8
		Nontypical	+ 37 3/8
Gross Score	457 2/8	Nontypical Score	449 7/8

CHAPTER 15

NUMBER 2 WORLD RECORD NONTYPICAL SHEDS

B&C 448 $^3/_8$

Dan Boles and a friend were out spring bear hunting. While in the bush, they always look for shed antlers. Dan spotted some white tips sticking up behind a log and told his friend that they looked like moose sheds. Upon getting to the log, they found the biggest elk antler they had ever seen. Due to its size and weight, Dan thought that the other side couldn't be very far away. Sure enough, eighty feet away lay the other side.

The antlers were measured and mounted, and at the time were the largest nontypical elk sheds ever found.

The following year, a large elk was found dead not far from where the sheds were found. It was the same animal. The big elk, known as the

Dan Boles.

Arrow Lake bull, is officially the new world record nontypical, scoring B&C 465 $^2/_8$ inches.

Using the same inside spread on the sheds, you can see they grew some seventeen inches in one year.

NUMBER 2 WORLD RECORD
NONTYPICAL SHEDS

Year: 1993
Hunter: Dan Boles

Location: British Columbia, Canada
Owner: Dan Boles

	Typical Points				Nontypical Points		
	Right Antler	Left Antler	Difference			Right Antler	Left Antler
Main Beam Length	50 6/8	46 6/8	4 0/8	1st Point		7 5/8	9 0/8
1st Point	24 0/8	23 6/8	2/8	2nd Point		4 0/8	16 1/8
2nd Point	21 7/8	23 3/8	1 4/8	3rd Point		4 4/8	
3rd Point	21 3/8	20 6/8	5/8	4th Point		1 4/8	
4th Point	21 7/8	21 0/8	7/8	5th Point		1 7/8	
5th Point	11 6/8	9 5/8	2 1/8	6th Point			
6th Point				7th Point			
7th Point				8th Point			
8th Point				9th Point			
1st Circumference	8 3/8	8 6/8	3/8	10th Point			
2nd Circumference	7 3/8	7 2/8	1/8	11th Point			
3rd Circumference	9 3/8	8 7/8	4/8	12th Point			
4th Circumference	9 1/8	9 5/8	4/8	13th Point			
				Subtotals		19 4/8	25 1/8
Total	185 7/8	179 6/8	10 7/8	Total		44 5/8	

DATA		TOTALS	
Number of Points Right	11	Inside Spread	49 0/8
Number of Points Left	8	Right Antler	185 7/8
Total Nontypical	44 5/8	Left Antler	179 6/8
Tip to Tip Spread	54 2/8	Typical Gross Score	414 5/8
Greatest Spread	63 5/8	Difference	-10 7/8
Inside Spread, Estimated	49 0/8	Typical Net Score	403 6/8
		Nontypical	+44 5/8
Gross Score	459 2/8	Nontypical Score	448 3/8

CHAPTER 16

COLORADO NONTYPICAL WITH THE MOST POINTS

B&C 447 $^2/_8$

This great bull was taken more than sixty years ago. Paul Dunn started the 101 Ranch (now the Rio Blanco Ranch) east of Meeker, Colorado, on the White River in 1922. It was there that he shot the elk in 1936.

Paul and his wife, Goldie, owned the Meeker Hotel from 1934 to 1964. The great bull has hung on the wall there ever since it was shot.

The rack cannot officially go into the Boone & Crockett record book because the skull was sawed in half, apparently to make it easier to pack out of the mountains.

The great bull possesses two remarkable features: It has the most points ever recorded on an elk—thirteen on each side—and it has 86 inches of abnormal measurement.

I find it intriguing to speculate on why hunters packed out some of these antlers but left many, many more in the mountains for the rodents to gnaw on.

Paul Dunn holds the mounted bull in front of the Meeker Hotel, late 1930s.

Tim Robertson and Bill Harlin taking bull off the wall for me to measure.

COLORADO NONTYPICAL WITH THE MOST POINTS

Year: 1936
Hunter: Paul Dunn

Location: Meeker, Colorado
Owner: Meeker Hotel & Cafe

	Typical Points				Nontypical Points	
	Right Antler	Left Antler	Difference		Right Antler	Left Antler
Main Beam Length	51 6/8	48 3/8	3 3/8	1st Point	16 0/8	11 4/8
1st Point	18 4/8	19 0/8	4/8	2nd Point	4 7/8	9 7/8
2nd Point	17 0/8	17 1/8	1/8	3rd Point	5 1/8	2 7/8
3rd Point	17 2/8	18 0/8	6/8	4th Point	2 0/8	11 6/8
4th Point	19 2/8	19 6/8	4/8	5th Point	4 0/8	4 6/8
5th Point	12 4/8	8 1/8	4 3/8	6th Point		10 5/8
6th Point	4 4/8	0	4 4/8	7th Point		2 7/8
7th Point	1 3/8	0	1 3/8	8th Point		
8th Point				9th Point		
1st Circumference	8 2/8	8 2/8	0	10th Point		
2nd Circumference	6 7/8	7 1/8	2/8	11th Point		
3rd Circumference	7 3/8	8 7/8	1 4/8	12th Point		
4th Circumference	7 1/8	8 4/8	1 3/8	13th Point		
				Subtotals	32 0/8	54 2/8
Total	171 6/8	163 1/8	18 5/8	Total	86 2/8	

DATA			TOTALS	
Number of Points Right	13		Inside Spread	44 6/8
Number of Points Left	13		Right Antler	171 6/8
Total Nontypical	86 2/8		Left Antler	163 1/8
Tip to Tip Spread	43 0/8		Typical Gross Score	379 5/8
Greatest Spread	59 3/8		Difference	-18 5/8
Inside Spread	44 6/8		Typical Net Score	361 0/8
			Nontypical	+86 2/8
Gross Score	465 7/8		*Nontypical Score	447 2/8

*Skull is cut, cannot be officially entered.

CHAPTER 17

FORMER WORLD RECORD NONTYPICAL

B&C 447 ¹/₈

BY BERRY BULL

Jim Berry had taken many elk over the years and was not searching for a trophy on that wintry day back in 1961.

"I was just after meat to feed my family," he says.

He was hunting north of Riding Mountain National Park in southwest Manitoba, in bushy flat land cut by a few ravines. He killed the animal with a single shot from his Winchester .30-30 carbine at about one hundred yards. The bull provided 560 pounds of meat.

It was only after moving to southwestern British Columbia that fellow Langley Rod and Gun Club members were able to see Jim's big elk rack. It was measured and sent to the Boone & Crockett Club's 21st Annual Awards program. At this event the rack was declared the world record nontypical. It held that ranking until 1998.

FORMER WORLD RECORD NONTYPICAL

Year: 1961
Hunter: James R. Berry

Location: Gilbert Plains, Manitoba, Canada
Owner: H&H Collection

	Typical Points				Nontypical Points	
	Right Antler	Left Antler	Difference		Right Antler	Left Antler
Main Beam Length	54 $^1/_8$	52 $^5/_8$	1 $^4/_8$	1st Point	4 $^6/_8$	26 $^7/_8$
1st Point	15 $^7/_8$	16 $^4/_8$	$^5/_8$	2nd Point	1 $^3/_8$	4 $^2/_8$
2nd Point	16 $^2/_8$	16 $^2/_8$	0	3rd Point		
3rd Point	28 $^2/_8$	24 $^4/_8$	3 $^6/_8$	4th Point		
4th Point	21 $^1/_8$	22 $^4/_8$	1 $^3/_8$	5th Point		
5th Point	18 $^5/_8$	20 $^0/_8$	1 $^3/_8$	6th Point		
6th Point	8 $^7/_8$	3 $^7/_8$	5 $^0/_8$	7th Point		
7th Point				8th Point		
8th Point				9th Point		
1st Circumference	11 $^0/_8$	10 $^2/_8$	$^6/_8$	10th Point		
2nd Circumference	7 $^1/_8$	7 $^1/_8$	0	11th Point		
3rd Circumference	7 $^1/_8$	7 $^1/_8$	0	12th Point		
4th Circumference	8 $^7/_8$	7 $^5/_8$	1 $^2/_8$	13th Point		
				Subtotals	6 $^1/_8$	31 $^1/_8$
Total	197 $^2/_8$	188 $^3/_8$	15 $^5/_8$	Total	37 $^2/_8$	

DATA		TOTALS	
Number of Points Right	9	Inside Spread	39 $^7/_8$
Number of Points Left	9	Right Antler	197 $^2/_8$
Total Nontypical	37 $^2/_8$	Left Antler	188 $^3/_8$
Tip to Tip Spread	45 $^1/_8$	Typical Gross Score	425 $^4/_8$
Greatest Spread	52 $^7/_8$	Difference	-15 $^5/_8$
Inside Spread	39 $^7/_8$	Typical Net Score	409 $^7/_8$
		Nontypical	+37 $^2/_8$
Gross Score	462 $^6/_8$	Nontypical Score	447 $^1/_8$

CHAPTER 18

NUMBER 3 WORLD RECORD
NONTYPICAL
SHEDS

B&C 443 ³/₈

These sheds were found in the Dry Lake region of Arizona's San Carlos Apache Reservation by tribal member Randal Johnson, He was out scouting for bear in the spring when he found the antlers about one hundred yards apart. Steve Stevens, a guide and avid elk hunter, bought the sheds from Randal and mounted them.

This is the second set of world-record class sheds found in the Dry Lake region. The other set was featured in the 1996 World Record Elk Tour and scored B&C 450 typical. If the points on this bull had not been broken in a fight, the rack would have a gross score of 480 inches nontypical. I would sure like to see the other bull in that fight!

From left: Paul Nosie Jr., Steve Stevens, and Roger Selner. In the background is my tour trailer.

NUMBER 3 WORLD RECORD NONTYPICAL SHEDS

Year: 1994

Location: San Carlos Apache Reservation, Arizona

Found by: Randal Johnson

Owner: Steve Stevens

	Typical Points				Nontypical Points	
	Right Antler	Left Antler	Difference		Right Antler	Left Antler
Main Beam Length	60 $^6/_8$	58 $^4/_8$	2 $^2/_8$	1st Point	15 $^0/_8$	13 $^0/_8$
1st Point	15 $^1/_8$	15 $^6/_8$	$^5/_8$	2nd Point		21 $^2/_8$
2nd Point	13 $^4/_8$	16 $^0/_8$	2 $^4/_8$	3rd Point		1 $^1/_8$
3rd Point	19 $^1/_8$	24 $^0/_8$	4 $^7/_8$	4th Point		
4th Point	21 $^0/_8$	18 $^0/_8$	3 $^0/_8$	5th Point		
5th Point	15 $^0/_8$	14 $^3/_8$	$^5/_8$	6th Point		
6th Point				7th Point		
7th Point				8th Point		
8th Point				9th Point		
1st Circumference	10 $^2/_8$	12 $^0/_8$	1 $^6/_8$	10th Point		
2nd Circumference	7 $^6/_8$	8 $^4/_8$	$^6/_8$	11th Point		
3rd Circumference	7 $^6/_8$	7 $^4/_8$	$^2/_8$	12th Point		
4th Circumference	7 $^3/_8$	7 $^6/_8$	$^3/_8$	13th Point		
				Subtotals	15 $^0/_8$	35 $^3/_8$
Total	177 $^5/_8$	182 $^3/_8$	20 $^0/_8$	Total	50 $^3/_8$	

DATA			TOTALS	
Number of Points Right	7		Inside Spread	53 $^0/_8$
Number of Points Left	9		Right Antler	177 $^5/_8$
Total Nontypical	50 $^3/_8$		Left Antler	182 $^3/_8$
Tip to Tip Spread	Unknown		Typical Gross Score	413 $^0/_8$
Greatest Spread	64 $^4/_8$		Difference	-20 $^0/_8$
Inside Spread, Estimated	53 $^0/_8$		Typical Net Score	393 $^0/_8$
			Nontypical	+50 $^3/_8$
Gross Score	463 $^3/_8$		Nontypical Score	443 $^3/_8$

CHAPTER 19

COLORADO STATE RECORD NONTYPICAL

B&C 441 ³/₈

This is another Meeker Hotel head. I have not been able to find any details on this elk, except that it has been in the hotel since at least the 1920s.

You can see in the pictures where it hung on the wall and the enormous size of the rack, with the huge drop tine that has a bulb on it. You can imagine how every time the bull turned its head, the rack could hit its body.

Don Stemler and I spent about two weeks at the hotel, measuring all the old heads. You can't see them in the photos, but there are some great mule deer heads in the hotel as well.

This shot was taken as I measured the bull. Note the old elk-antler chair in the background.

This bull was placed on the wall at the Meeker Hotel.

COLORADO STATE RECORD NONTYPICAL

Year: Prior to 1930
Hunter: Unknown

Location: Meeker, Colorado Area
Owner: Meeker Hotel & Cafe

	Typical Points				Nontypical Points		
	Right Antler	Left Antler	Difference			Right Antler	Left Antler
Main Beam Length	51 4/8	54 1/8	2 5/8	1st Point		1 4/8	25 4/8
1st Point	16 6/8	15 4/8	1 2/8	2nd Point		1 1/8	8 0/8
2nd Point	14 6/8	16 1/8	1 3/8	3rd Point		1 6/8	6 4/8
3rd Point	10 2/8	11 4/8	1 2/8	4th Point		1 3/8	
4th Point	18 0/8	18 4/8	4/8	5th Point		2 0/8	
5th Point	13 6/8	15 6/8	2 0/8	6th Point		15 0/8	
6th Point				7th Point		4 0/8	
7th Point				8th Point		13 0/8	
8th Point				9th Point			
1st Circumference	9 7/8	10 2/8	3/8	10th Point			
2nd Circumference	7 2/8	7 1/8	1/8	11th Point			
3rd Circumference	7 1/8	7 6/8	5/8	12th Point			
4th Circumference	10 0/8	10 5/8	5/8	13th Point			
				Subtotals		39 6/8	40 0/8
Total	159 2/8	167 2/8	10 6/8	Total		79 6/8	

DATA		TOTALS	
Number of Points Right	14	Inside Spread	45 7/8
Number of Points Left	9	Right Antler	159 2/8
Total Nontypical	79 6/8	Left Antler	167 2/8
Tip to Tip Spread	35 2/8	Typical Gross Score	372 3/8
Greatest Spread	50 6/8	Difference	-10 6/8
Inside Spread	45 7/8	Typical Net Score	361 5/8
		Nontypical	+79 6/8
Gross Score	452 1/8	*Nontypical Score	441 3/8

Score pending verification from awards program in summer 2001.

CHAPTER 20

NUMBER 4 WORLD RECORD
NONTYPICAL
SHEDS

B&C 439 $^0/_8$

This great set of antlers was found by two different shed hunters in the spring of 1980. Later that year, Mannie Moore, an antler collector in Montana, traded some whitetails for the elk antlers and paired them up.

Again, with some of these great antlers, the only proof of the animal's existence is a set of shed antlers that it left in the mountains.

Jean Moore holding antlers.

NUMBER 4 WORLD RECORD NONTYPICAL SHEDS

Year: 1980
Found by: Unknown

Location: Cabinet Mountains, Montana
Owner: H&H Collection

	Typical Points				Nontypical Points	
	Right Antler	Left Antler	Difference		Right Antler	Left Antler
Main Beam Length	49 5/8	48 4/8	1 1/8	1st Point	2 5/8	3 6/8
1st Point	16 4/8	15 6/8	6/8	2nd Point	2 7/8	3 2/8
2nd Point	19 7/8	21 4/8	1 5/8	3rd Point	24 2/8	9 2/8
3rd Point	24 7/8	22 4/8	2 3/8	4th Point		20 4/8
4th Point	17 0/8	17 4/8	4/8	5th Point		
5th Point	10 4/8	18 0/8	7 4/8	6th Point		
6th Point	2 7/8	0	2 7/8	7th Point		
7th Point				8th Point		
8th Point				9th Point		
1st Circumference	9 3/8	9 1/8	2/8	10th Point		
2nd Circumference	7 0/8	6 7/8	1/8	11th Point		
3rd Circumference	6 1/8	7 2/8	1 1/8	12th Point		
4th Circumference	6 7/8	11 2/8	4 3/8	13th Point		
				Subtotals	29 6/8	36 6/8
Total	170 3/8	178 2/8	22 5/8	Total	66 4/8	

DATA		TOTALS	
Number of Points Right	10	Inside Spread	46 4/8
Number of Points Left	10	Right Antler	170 3/8
Total Nontypical	66 4/8	Left Antler	178 2/8
Tip to Tip Spread	51 0/8	Typical Gross Score	395 1/8
Greatest Spread	57 6/8	Difference	-22 5/8
Inside Spread, Estimated	46 4/8	Typical Net Score	372 4/8
		Nontypical	+66 4/8
Gross Score	461 5/8	Nontypical Score	439 0/8

CHAPTER 21

NUMBER 5 WORLD RECORD NONTYPICAL

B&C 432 ⁵/₈

Game officials on Arizona's San Carlos Apache Reservation manage some of the largest elk in North America, so Nathaniel Boni had a chance to get a big bull, thanks to drawing a limited trophy tag for the reservation.

He saw his trophy while looking over a group of bulls—but didn't recognize it. Looking at the bull from the front and thinking it was a narrow, young five-point, he decided not to shoot. Then the bull turned its head. Wow! It showed long beams and a lot of points, a trophy of a lifetime.

NUMBER 5 WORLD RECORD NONTYPICAL

Year: 1994

Location: San Carlos Apache Reservation, Arizona

Hunter: Nathaniel Boni

Owner: Alan Ellsworth

	Typical Points				Nontypical Points	
	Right Antler	Left Antler	Difference		Right Antler	Left Antler
Main Beam Length	56 7/8	57 3/8	4/8	1st Point	16 7/8	3 3/8
1st Point	17 0/8	17 1/8	1/8	2nd Point		4 2/8
2nd Point	17 6/8	20 2/8	2 4/8	3rd Point		
3rd Point	23 7/8	24 3/8	4/8	4th Point		
4th Point	20 3/8	18 2/8	2 1/8	5th Point		
5th Point	18 2/8	15 6/8	2 4/8	6th Point		
6th Point	7 3/8	7 1/8	2/8	7th Point		
7th Point				8th Point		
8th Point				9th Point		
1st Circumference	9 6/8	9 7/8	1/8	10th Point		
2nd Circumference	6 6/8	6 7/8	1/8	11th Point		
3rd Circumference	6 3/8	6 6/8	3/8	12th Point		
4th Circumference	6 7/8	8 2/8	1 3/8	13th Point		
				Subtotals	16 7/8	7 5/8
Total	191 2/8	192 0/8	10 4/8	Total	24 4/8	

DATA		TOTALS	
Number of Points Right	8	Inside Spread	35 1/8
Number of Points Left	9	Right Antler	191 2/8
Total Nontypical	24 4/8	Left Antler	192 0/8
Tip to Tip Spread	22 1/8	Typical Gross Score	418 5/8
Greatest Spread	47 2/8	Difference	-10 4/8
Inside Spread	35 3/8	Typical Net Score	408 1/8
		Nontypical	+24 4/8
Gross Score	443 1/8	Nontypical Score	432 5/8

CHAPTER 22

MONTANA STATE RECORD NONTYPICAL (UNOFFICIAL)

B&C 432 $^3/_8$

BY J. J. LAMB

Grandfather George Lamb rescued this huge set of antlers from the Scratchgravel Landfill in Helena, Montana, more than sixty years ago. After grandfather died, my father, John, moved the unique antlers to his Helena home, where they languished along a fence next to the woodshed. My dad, brother, and I always thought they were a nice set of antlers, but they just sat out in the back of my dad's house.

My brother, Duke, tried to tack the rack onto the woodshed, but they fell off and the skull broke in two. The antlers lay there for years. Finally, in June of 1998, I decided to take them to a taxidermist for mounting. My family was going to split the bill three ways.

My family has hunted elk for years, but no one has ever taken an animal with antlers the size of my grandfather's find. We have never been big on mounting things; we're pretty much just meat hunters. My dad always had that old-time philosophy about how you couldn't eat the horns.

Roger Selner from the Eastmans' World Record Elk Tour heard about the rack and took care of the cost of having them mounted so they could be displayed in the tour. The antlers cannot officially go into the record book because of the cracked skull, but their score would exceed the current Montana record by nine inches.

John Thomas holds the rack before it was restored. With him is Mac Vosbeck.

John Thomas and Montana record bull.

MONTANA STATE RECORD
NONTYPICAL (UNOFFICIAL)

Year: Prior to 1938   **Location:** Helena, Montana
Found by: George Lamb   **Owner:** The Lamb Family

	Typical Points				Nontypical Points	
	Right Antler	Left Antler	Difference		Right Antler	Left Antler
Main Beam Length	57 1/8	54 6/8	2 3/8	1st Point	1 4/8	1 2/8
1st Point	17 5/8	16 6/8	7/8	2nd Point	5 0/8	11 7/8
2nd Point	20 0/8	18 4/8	1 4/8	3rd Point	13 0/8	
3rd Point	13 2/8	14 4/8	1 2/8	4th Point	5 5/8	
4th Point	21 6/8	17 2/8	4 4/8	5th Point		
5th Point	18 4/8	16 6/8	1 6/8	6th Point		
6th Point	10 6/8	5 0/8	5 6/8	7th Point		
7th Point				8th Point		
8th Point				9th Point		
1st Circumference	10 3/8	10 0/8	3/8	10th Point		
2nd Circumference	7 6/8	7 6/8	0	11th Point		
3rd Circumference	7 2/8	6 7/8	3/8	12th Point		
4th Circumference	8 1/8	8 7/8	6/8	13th Point		
				Subtotals	25 1/8	13 1/8
Total	192 4/8	177 0/8	19 4/8	Total	38 2/8	

DATA		TOTALS	
Number of Points Right	11	Inside Spread	44 1/8
Number of Points Left	9	Right Antler	192 4/8
Total Nontypical	38 2/8	Left Antler	177 0/8
Tip to Tip Spread	41 2/8	Typical Gross Score	413 5/8
Greatest Spread	53 1/8	Difference	-19 4/8
Inside Spread, Estimated	44 1/8	Typical Net Score	394 1/8
		Nontypical	+38 2/8
Gross Score	451 5/8	*Nontypical Score	432 3/8

*Skull was cracked, cannot officially be entered.

NUMBER 2 WORLD RECORD NONTYPICAL ARCHERY

P&Y 417 0/8

ARIZONA DREAMING
BY BRADY J. DUPKE

With breathless anticipation, I slowly opened the mailbox and ripped open the letter. There it was! I had drawn a coveted northern Arizona archery bull elk permit. In reality, half the battle was in obtaining a permit, because only one hundred tags are allotted for this unit. I had been lucky enough to have drawn a permit for the same area the previous year, so I knew the unit well. Some of the bulls I had bugled in and seen that year were huge!

Unfortunately, I had not connected with the bull of my dreams and had settled for a smaller five-point. This time I was determined to bag a real trophy bull or go home empty-handed. Equally fortunate in drawing a tag were my two good hunting friends, Ric Chaudoin and Ron Pickering.

We'd hunted together for the previous ten years; in fact, they have taken me hunting ever since I was twelve years old.

The unit I had drawn is in the Arizona high country. It ranges from towering pines to pinyon pine and junipers and then drops down into sagebrush flats. Elk occupy all areas of the unit, thanks to the abundance of domestic livestock water tanks. Access to the area is by primitive dirt roads, and the land tends to be fairly flat, giving you the opportunity to cover a variety of different country in a short amount of time.

Before the hunt, we spent several weekends scouting for trophy-class bulls. At night we would drive the roads and periodically stop and bugle to find concentrations of bulls. Our efforts were often rewarded. During the day we checked the water tanks for any fresh, large bull tracks. Late afternoons and early evenings were spent glassing open meadows, hoping to find herd bulls. After several weeks of scouting, we decided on a central location for our base camp. The area contained several bulls that we thought would score over 350 points.

Finally, opening day of the hunt arrived; I had fourteen glorious days to bag a trophy bull. We decided to split up—Ric and Ron would stay together, and I would go after a bull I had spotted the previous evening. At 3:30 A.M. I took off on my four-wheeler so I could arrive well before daylight. The herd bull (which I guessed would score 380) and his cows had watered before sunup and were heading for thicker cover to bed down. I bugled and he responded, but there was no turning him away from his coveted cows. In the meantime, my calling had successfully attracted two six-point satellite bulls, but neither was big enough. Ric and Ron had similar luck that day. Both had opportunities to take smaller elk but decided to pass up the shots.

The perfect hunting weather held for the next several days. The cold, brisk mornings seemed to heighten the elk's rutting behavior. Bulls were bugling almost in a frenzy, and we all had to force ourselves to pass up average animals and wait for "the big one."

On day four, Ric and Ron had the hunting experience of a lifetime. Shortly after dawn, they were working two six-point bulls that were fighting over a herd of cows. They quietly slipped in between the cows and the bulls and then let out a bugle. The challenge enraged both bulls so much that they ran over a small rise to greet the intruder. Ron took a frontal shot and arrowed one of the bulls directly in the jugular vein. The elk took off, but Ron knew he had his bull. In the meantime, Ric's elk charged to within twenty yards, giving him a perfect broadside shot, and he put his arrow through both lungs. The whole episode took less than sixty seconds. Not bad for two guys on their first archery bull hunt.

Both beautiful six-points scored well into the Pope and Young record book. As for me, I was still off searching for my dream elk.

The next day, my partner, Todd Ralls, arrived for moral and hunting support. Ric and Ron were determined to stay as long as it took for me to bag an elk. For the next several days the good weather continued, and we decided to split up into pairs to search for "my" elk. On the ninth day, Ric and Ron came back to camp with a story about a bull that was unbelievable. According to them, it would easily score over 400. Frankly, I had to see this huge elk for myself before I'd believe it.

Early the next morning, Todd and I set off for the area where they had spotted the bull. At the first bugle I let out, at least four bulls responded. I didn't know which way to go! As daylight broke, I found a beautiful seven-point bull feeding in a meadow with his cows. I used every available patch of cover and inched my way downwind of them. When I was within one hundred yards, I let out another bugle to see if I could coax him away from the herd. He wouldn't budge. Todd suggested we rake a tree with a stick to see if it might anger him. The effort was futile; the bull ignored us and slowly gathered his cows, herding them toward thicker cover.

I decided to hike slowly around to the other side of the timber and get in front of the herd. Hidden under a tree, I could hear the big bull bugling his way down a fence line toward me. One by one, the cows walked by no more than ten yards away, and I could see the bull bringing up the rear. This was it. I just knew it. He was mine! The bull came within five yards, but instead of following the cows, he went behind a large cedar tree. He took one look at me, but I didn't have a clear shot and the rest was history. So go the best-laid plans.

Frustrated beyond belief, Todd and I sat down. Suddenly, another bull bugled below us, and we were on our feet instantly. This new bull had been following the herd and apparently did not have any cows of his own. I immediately cow-called, and he began to work his way toward us. I set up about fifteen yards in front of Todd and let him do the cow-calling. The bull walked within bow range, but I couldn't get a clear shot because of the thick cover. Finally, he winded us and promptly vacated the country. Oh well, just another 350-point bull to tell my friends about. After all this aggravation, we decided to take a break and go into town to clean up and regroup for the evening hunt.

Late afternoon found us back in the same area, still searching for that so-called 400-plus "dream bull" that Ric and Ron had supposedly spotted. Our first bugle resulted in an immediate response. This bull was so furious that he nearly ran over us! I was ready, my bow was drawn, and I had a clear shot. One look was all it took; he was a story in himself. His right antler was a beautiful six-point, but his left antler was "nightmared," sporting only one eye guard and two main beams. Not exactly my dream bull.

Within the next minute, we heard a bugle beyond the ridge that shook the woods. Cautiously, Todd and I stalked over the hill and commenced glassing. We immediately spotted a very large herd of cows but couldn't see the bull. All of a sudden, over the ridge came a gigantic set of antlers and attached to them was the largest elk I'd ever seen. Now we knew Ric and Ron hadn't been telling cock-and-bull stories.

We were about one hundred fifty yards away at this point. The wind was perfect, and the bull was busy raking and thrashing a tree. He was making so much noise that I knew he would not hear me while I closed the distance. His cows were feeding off to the right and had moved into a draw. I had to get between him and his cows before he came looking for them. I made the stalk without him seeing me, and, as if on cue, he walked out of the trees and gave me a fifty-yard, broadside shot. I remember aiming, praying, and releasing the arrow. Smack! I hit him, but not exactly where I had planned. The arrow hit too far back for a one-shot kill, and he took off like a runaway freight train. Now it was decision time; dusk had fallen, and it was getting darker by the minute. I knew a gut-shot animal would lie down as soon as possible. I reluctantly decided to flag the spot and come back at first light.

That was the longest night of my life. Todd and I waited at camp until there was enough light to see, and then started tracking the bull from my "flagged" spot. The trail was easy to follow for the first two hundred yards because we could see his tracks. There wasn't any blood, though, and my heart began to sink as we found fewer and fewer tracks.

We decided to split up. Todd would try to follow the tracks while I circled out ahead of him. I knew the bull would be looking for a sheltered spot to bed down, so I searched for the thickest area I could find. Out of

Brady Dupke with No. 2 archery nontypical.

the corner of my eye I caught a slight movement in a jackpine thicket. I threw my binoculars up and spotted antlers weaving back and forth.

He was alive, but apparently very sick. I nocked an arrow and crept slowly downwind of the thicket. When I was within twenty yards, I slowly raised my bow and pulled the bowstring back. I didn't have a clear shot at any of the bull's vitals. He must have heard me, because he instantly jumped to his feet and ran. I could tell he was in pretty bad shape. Trying to keep him in sight, I followed until finally he turned and gave me the broadside shot I needed. I held my breath as I placed my thirty-yard pin behind his shoulder. This time I was right on the money, a perfect double-lung shot. He bolted twenty yards and piled up. I yelled at the top of my lungs for Todd, who was still looking for tracks, to get over here. He ran over as fast as he could, and we both stood and breathlessly gazed at my trophy bull elk.

I shot the bull on the eleventh day of the hunt in September of 1993. He has an impressive 8x7 rack and is the pending Pope and Young world record bull elk (nontypical category) with an official score of 421 $7/8$ points. His main beams are 56 inches long, and he has an inside antler spread of 52 $1/2$ inches.

The bull was definitely worth the wait. I had passed up several trophy bulls and my patience and persistence had paid off. Not bad for a twenty-two-year-old kid from Arizona.

I killed my bull with a High Country Safari Bow set at 82 pounds. I used Easton's 2413xx 75s tipped with Thunderhead 100s.

NUMBER 2 WORLD RECORD NONTYPICAL ARCHERY

Year: 1993
Hunter: Brady Dupke

Location: Coconino County, Arizona
Owner: Brady Dupke

	Typical Points				Nontypical Points	
	Right Antler	Left Antler	Difference		Right Antler	Left Antler
Main Beam Length	56 0/8	56 1/8	1/8	1st Point	1 4/8	8 1/8
1st Point	16 4/8	17 7/8	1 3/8	2nd Point	16 0/8	
2nd Point	18 5/8	19 4/8	7/8	3rd Point		
3rd Point	17 2/8	16 0/8	1 2/8	4th Point		
4th Point	20 4/8	21 5/8	1 1/8	5th Point		
5th Point	13 3/8	16 2/8	2 7/8	6th Point		
6th Point				7th Point		
7th Point				8th Point		
8th Point				9th Point		
1st Circumference	8 5/8	8 4/8	1/8	10th Point		
2nd Circumference	6 7/8	6 7/8	0	11th Point		
3rd Circumference	6 5/8	6 7/8	2/8	12th Point		
4th Circumference	6 6/8	7 4/8	6/8	13th Point		
				Subtotals	17 4/8	8 1/8
Total	171 1/8	177 1/8	8 6/8	Total	25 5/8	

DATA		TOTALS	
Number of Points Right	8	Inside Spread	51 7/8
Number of Points Left	7	Right Antler	171 1/8
Total Nontypical	25 5/8	Left Antler	177 1/8
Tip to Tip Spread	52 1/8	Typical Gross Score	400 1/8
Greatest Spread	52 6/8	Difference	-8 6/8
Inside Spread	51 7/8	Typical Net Score	391 3/8
		Nontypical	+25 5/8
Gross Score	425 6/8	Nontypical Score	417 0/8

CHAPTER 24

NUMBER 5 ARIZONA STATE RECORD NONTYPICAL

B&C 417 ⁰/₈

Arizona has produced another giant bull elk! The huge nontypical that was officially scored at 427 ¹/₈ by measurer Robin Bechtel has an extra, nonmatching point on the right antler, making it nontypical.

If the left antler also had an extra point, the bull would score over 442 typical, possibly a new world record. This would be an entry score, of course, and the head would have to be panel-measured to determine its final score. Any trophy ranking in the top ten is required to be measured by a panel of judges.

On 7 December 1993, Tim Pender, wildlife manager for the Arizona Game and Fish Department's Region III, was accompanying his fourteen-year-old son, Tommy, on an elk hunt in Coconino County. On the fifth day of their hunt, the

Penders found the dead bull. The carcass had been completely cleaned of all meat, indicating the bull had been dead for several months. They studied the carcass for some time, but the cause of death could not be determined. "If this bull lost a fight with a bigger one, I sure would like to see the winner!" Tim remarked.

A short time later, Tommy got his first elk; now they had two trophies to pack out.

Tim Pender found these antlers in Arizona in December 1993.

NUMBER 5 ARIZONA STATE RECORD NONTYPICAL

Year: 1993
Found by: Tim Pender

Location: Coconino County, Arizona
Owner: Tim Pender

	Typical Points				Nontypical Points	
	Right Antler	Left Antler	Difference		Right Antler	Left Antler
Main Beam Length	57 5/8	56 5/8	1 0/8	1st Point	20 6/8	0
1st Point	17 2/8	16 3/8	7/8	2nd Point		
2nd Point	17 2/8	18 1/8	7/8	3rd Point		
3rd Point	10 7/8	14 3/8	3 4/8	4th Point		
4th Point	25 5/8	26 0/8	3/8	5th Point		
5th Point	16 5/8	16 4/8	1/8	6th Point		
6th Point				7th Point		
7th Point				8th Point		
8th Point				9th Point		
1st Circumference	10 6/8	9 6/8	1 0/8	10th Point		
2nd Circumference	7 3/8	7 5/8	2/8	11th Point		
3rd Circumference	8 4/8	7 5/8	7/8	12th Point		
4th Circumference	6 2/8	5 7/8	3/8	13th Point		
				Subtotals	20 6/8	0
Total	178 1/8	178 7/8	9 2/8	Total	20 6/8	

DATA		TOTALS	
Number of Points Right	7	Inside Spread	48 4/8
Number of Points Left	6	Right Antler	178 1/8
Total Nontypical	20 6/8	Left Antler	178 7/8
Tip to Tip Spread	50 5/8	Typical Gross Score	405 4/8
Greatest Spread	50 6/8	Difference	-9 2/8
Inside Spread	48 4/8	Typical Net Score	396 2/8
		Nontypical	+20 6/8
Gross Score	426 2/8	Nontypical Score	417 0/8

CHAPTER 25

NEVADA STATE RECORD
NONTYPICAL
SHEDS

B&C 415 ⁵/₈

Ron Hulse and his friend Kurt Ludlow are avid hunters, and one of their favorite pastimes is looking for shed antlers. While on a trip to Nevada in 1998, they found a large ten-point elk shed. It was one of the largest antlers they had ever found, and they were determined to find the other side.

It was not an easy task. But after two days of walking over many miles, patterning the area, they found the other side about one hundred yards from where they had found the first side.

Two weeks later Kurt went back to the same area to look for more antlers. He found a pair of elk sheds together. After he and Ron compared them to the first set, they determined both sets were from the same bull. The largest set (1996—shown here) scores 415 $^5/_8$. The second set (1997) scores in the 390s. This lower score may be due to old age, drought conditions, or food supply during the season.

The 1998 season antlers from this bull were not found. The bull, if harvested, would rank at about No. 4 in Nevada.

Kurt Ludlow, left, holds the 1997 set and Ron Hulse the 1996 set.

NEVADA STATE RECORD NONTYPICAL SHEDS

Year: 1996　　　　　　　　　　　　　**Location: Nevada**
Found by: Ron Hulse and Kurt Ludlow　**Owner: Ron Hulse and Kurt Ludlow**

	Typical Points				Nontypical Points	
	Right Antler	Left Antler	Difference		Right Antler	Left Antler
Main Beam Length	49 $^5/_8$	52 $^5/_8$	3 $^0/_8$	1st Point	1 $^4/_8$	1 $^5/_8$
1st Point	16 $^4/_8$	16 $^0/_8$	$^4/_8$	2nd Point	9 $^7/_8$	8 $^3/_8$
2nd Point	20 $^0/_8$	19 $^3/_8$	$^5/_8$	3rd Point		13 $^6/_8$
3rd Point	18 $^4/_8$	18 $^6/_8$	$^2/_8$	4th Point		
4th Point	21 $^3/_8$	21 $^0/_8$	$^3/_8$	5th Point		
5th Point	17 $^1/_8$	17 $^0/_8$	$^1/_8$	6th Point		
6th Point	4 $^7/_8$	1 $^6/_8$	3 $^1/_8$	7th Point		
7th Point				8th Point		
8th Point				9th Point		
1st Circumference	9 $^3/_8$	9 $^6/_8$	$^3/_8$	10th Point		
2nd Circumference	6 $^6/_8$	7 $^1/_8$	$^3/_8$	11th Point		
3rd Circumference	6 $^4/_8$	6 $^4/_8$	0	12th Point		
4th Circumference	5 $^6/_8$	6 $^2/_8$	$^4/_8$	13th Point		
				Subtotals	11 $^3/_8$	23 $^6/_8$
Total	176 $^3/_8$	176 $^1/_8$	9 $^0/_8$	Total	35 $^1/_8$	

DATA		TOTALS	
Number of Points Right	9	Inside Spread	37 $^0/_8$
Number of Points Left	10	Right Antler	176 $^3/_8$
Total Nontypical	35 $^1/_8$	Left Antler	176 $^1/_8$
Tip to Tip Spread	Unknown	Typical Gross Score	389 $^4/_8$
Greatest Spread	59 $^0/_8$	Difference	-9 $^0/_8$
Inside Spread, Estimated	37 $^0/_8$	Typical Net Score	380 $^4/_8$
		Nontypical	+35 $^1/_8$
Gross Score	424 $^5/_8$	Nontypical Score	415 $^5/_8$

CHAPTER 26

WYOMING STATE RECORD NONTYPICAL

B&C 415 $^2/_8$

**AS TOLD TO THE AUTHOR
BY ROD M. ODENBACH**

Rod M. Odenbach is an avid outdoorsman. He enjoys taking his family fishing, hunting, and looking for arrowheads. One of their favorite springtime sports is going out and looking for shed antlers. In fact, this activity has become quite a competition between Rod, his son, Michael, and a friend of theirs, Scott Hokanson.

In the spring of 1992, Rod found a large pair of elk sheds on a ranch where he had hunted. Rod's desire to take a record-book bull increased after finding the sheds. Given the normal growth of elk antlers, the bull that year of the find would have been close to making Boone & Crockett's minimum requirements.

That fall, Rod was booked up with his outfitting business and couldn't find the time to get out himself and hunt. The following spring, they looked for the bull sheds again. They found some good ones, but not the same bull's. Rod put in for the same elk unit and drew a tag.

Archery season found Rod and Scott looking for the monster bull. They tracked several big elk, but had no luck in finding their elusive target.

Rifle season came, and finally, on 10 November, Rod and Scott headed to the Big Horn Mountains to check out several of their favorite hunting spots. After glassing for a while, they spotted tracks in one of the drainages, so they crossed to the other side. There they found six sets of tracks, including one big bull track. The sight of it filled them with excitement.

Glassing ahead, they watched the small bunch cross the canyon. Rod waited until the big bull stepped out. He fired one shot from his Dakota Arms .270, and the big elk lunged into the timber. They tracked it for one hundred yards, and a second shot by Rod at fifty yards finished the job.

Scott and Rod spent 8½ hours packing the bull out. They estimated it weighed between 850 and 900 pounds. A retired Wyoming game and fish official estimated the bull's age at about twelve years. The bull had grown more than twenty inches of antler on each side in two years.

The great elk was measured at the Boone & Crockett Club's 22nd Big Game Awards Program in 1995 in Dallas, Texas.

Wyoming state record nontypical: B&C 415 2/8. Taken in Johnson County, Wyoming, by Rod Odenbach, 1993.

Rod Odenbach with sheds off bull taken in 1993. Wyoming State Record Nontypical 415 2/8.

WYOMING STATE RECORD NONTYPICAL

Year: 1993   **Location:** Johnson County, Wyoming
Hunter: Rod M. Odenbach   **Owner:** Rod M. Odenbach

	Typical Points				Nontypical Points	
	Right Antler	Left Antler	Difference		Right Antler	Left Antler
Main Beam Length	54 ^{0}/$_8$	55 ^{0}/$_8$	1 ^{0}/$_8$	1st Point	1 ^{3}/$_8$	1 ^{5}/$_8$
1st Point	17 ^{0}/$_8$	16 ^{2}/$_8$	^{6}/$_8$	2nd Point		
2nd Point	20 ^{1}/$_8$	18 ^{4}/$_8$	1 ^{5}/$_8$	3rd Point		
3rd Point	16 ^{6}/$_8$	16 ^{5}/$_8$	^{1}/$_8$	4th Point		
4th Point	25 ^{2}/$_8$	26 ^{2}/$_8$	1 ^{0}/$_8$	5th Point		
5th Point	18 ^{4}/$_8$	20 ^{3}/$_8$	1 ^{7}/$_8$	6th Point		
6th Point	6 ^{4}/$_8$	6 ^{5}/$_8$	^{1}/$_8$	7th Point		
7th Point				8th Point		
8th Point				9th Point		
1st Circumference	8 ^{7}/$_8$	9 ^{4}/$_8$	^{5}/$_8$	10th Point		
2nd Circumference	6 ^{4}/$_8$	6 ^{5}/$_8$	^{1}/$_8$	11th Point		
3rd Circumference	6 ^{7}/$_8$	6 ^{7}/$_8$	0	12th Point		
4th Circumference	7 ^{1}/$_8$	6 ^{7}/$_8$	^{2}/$_8$	13th Point		
				Subtotals	1 ^{3}/$_8$	1 ^{5}/$_8$
Total	187 ^{4}/$_8$	189 ^{4}/$_8$	7 ^{4}/$_8$	Total	3 ^{0}/$_8$	

DATA		TOTALS	
Number of Points Right	8	Inside Spread	42 ^{6}/$_8$
Number of Points Left	8	Right Antler	187 ^{4}/$_8$
Total Nontypical	3 ^{0}/$_8$	Left Antler	189 ^{4}/$_8$
Tip to Tip Spread	36 ^{2}/$_8$	Typical Gross Score	419 ^{6}/$_8$
Greatest Spread	52 ^{0}/$_8$	Difference	-7 ^{4}/$_8$
Inside Spread	42 ^{6}/$_8$	Typical Net Score	412 ^{2}/$_8$
		Nontypical	+3 ^{0}/$_8$
Gross Score	422 ^{6}/$_8$	Nontypical Score	415 ^{2}/$_8$

NUMBER 2 NEW MEXICO STATE RECORD NONTYPICAL

B&C 414 0/8

BY LOU A. DEPAOLIS

The hunt for Lou DePaolis's nontypical American elk took place on the famed Vermejo Ranch in northern New Mexico in 1974. However, the story actually began in New York State, where Lou and his hunting companions still live.

Lou's regular hunting partners include Don Peters (brother-in-law), Don Moyer, and Bill Richardson, a former guide in British Columbia and Quebec. Lou made all the arrangements for their 1974 hunt, and they left for New Mexico on a Friday in October after everyone got off work. At their designated meeting area, the four men made one last check of their equipment and then headed west at 5 P.M. The party took two pickup trucks, one a 4x4 for getting into the more difficult hunting areas and the other a standard pickup.

Two men went in each truck, alternately sleeping and driving all the first night. They had breakfast the next morning in Indiana, then continued on to Texas, where they spent their second night. After a well-deserved night's sleep and a hefty breakfast, they headed for Raton, New Mexico, and continued on to the ranch headquarters, where they checked in.

Once they were signed in, Lou and his companions were on their own. They took the back roads into their assigned high-country hunt area. The elevation of the ranch starts at 6,500 feet and goes to well over 9,000 feet at State Line Cabin, which they used as their base camp. The cabin is one hundred yards from the Colorado border on Vermejo Creek.

According to Lou, Vermejo Creek is the key secret to hunting Vermejo Ranch. When the weather gets bad, elk migrate along the creek to their wintering grounds.

Lou's party usually splits up and hunts in pairs. Each day they switch companions and go to a different area, where they bugle and evaluate the trophies that respond to their calling. Lou's group learned many years earlier that the herd bull wasn't necessarily the one they were after. Sometimes older bulls that have been drummed out of the herds are the bigger animals.

On this day Lou hunted with Bill Richardson in the Costilla Meadow area. Late in the afternoon they positioned themselves on a hummock to glass the area before nightfall. They had already looked over a couple of herds that had 5x5 bulls, but passed them up because they were looking for 6x6 animals.

Bill was glassing through a spotting scope, and Lou, about ten feet to Bill's left, was looking down a draw when he spotted a small herd of elk near the tree line. He evaluated them and determined that the bull was a nice 6x6. He got ready to take it, but as Lou was positioning himself, Bill whispered excitedly, "Get over here right now!" The tone of voice told Lou that Bill had spotted something exceptional, and he rolled over and took a look through the spotting scope. Lou whispered. "It looks like a darn caribou."

The bull was so big that Lou did not believe it when Bill told him it was over four hundred yards away. Lou got in a comfortable position to shoot and touched off the first round. The cows and the big bull milled around, trying to decide which way to go. Apparently they couldn't determine where the shot had come from.

Bill told Lou that he had missed—the bullet had hit right at the bull's feet. By this time it was getting dark and Lou was having a hard time isolating the bull again. Suddenly, the bull presented itself well, and Lou touched off a second shot, aiming a little higher. At the crack of the rifle, all the elk disappeared and the meadow was empty.

Bill was upset and told Lou he had missed the big bull again. Lou marked the bull's last position near a large tree. All the way to that spot, Bill kept telling Lou that he had missed.

When they got to the site, Bill told Lou it was 437 paces. By then it was almost pitch dark. They were groping their way from tree to tree when Lou tripped right over his bull. He never had such a thrill in his life. Bill, a big guy

and usually calm, grabbed Lou and threw him up in the air in his excitement.

Lou was reluctant to leave his trophy, but Bill insisted they had to go back and get some lights and help before they could get the animal out of the field. Eventually, Bill convinced Lou he knew exactly where they were and that they could find his trophy again. They hiked the half-mile back to the pickup truck in record time and drove back to the cabin. There they got their lights and hunting companions and returned to dress the animal.

Not only was Lou successful on this hunt, so was everyone else in his hunting party. Don Peters took a tremendous 7x7 trophy, and Don Moyer and Bill Richardson each took a respectable 6x6 bull. The excitement and success of their

Left to right: Bill Richardson, Don Moyer, Don Peters and Lou DePaolis with his record elk.

hunt helped keep Lou and his friends awake on the return drive home.

Originally published in the Boone & Crockett Club's 20th Big Game Awards: 1986–1988. Reprinted with permission.

Notes: Lou DePaolis's elk was the New Mexico state record nontypical from 1974 until 1992, when Martin Huggins shot a B&C 417 6/8 nontypical.

If you look at Lou's field photo of his bull, you will see that the large nontypical point on the right antler between the fourth and fifth point was broken off. It is in the same location as the big forked nontypical point on the left antler. I estimate that a total of about fourteen inches were broken off.

Lou's first elk is indeed a great one. It looks like it would score B&C 375 to 380.

Lou DePaolis with his trophy elk, October 1974

NUMBER 2 NEW MEXICO STATE RECORD NONTYPICAL

Year: 1974
Hunter: Lou A. DePaolis

Location: Taos County, New Mexico
Owner: Bass Pro Wildlife Museum

	Typical Points				Nontypical Points	
	Right Antler	Left Antler	Difference		Right Antler	Left Antler
Main Beam Length	48 2/8	48 2/8	0	1st Point	2 6/8	4 5/8
1st Point	23 6/8	20 0/8	3 6/8	2nd Point	3 0/8	9 2/8
2nd Point	16 6/8	18 3/8	1 5/8	3rd Point	4 6/8	4 6/8
3rd Point	20 0/8	20 5/8	5/8	4th Point		8 2/8
4th Point	21 2/8	20 1/8	1 1/8	5th Point		
5th Point	13 3/8	13 0/8	3/8	6th Point		
6th Point				7th Point		
7th Point				8th Point		
8th Point				9th Point		
1st Circumference	7 3/8	6 5/8	6/8	10th Point		
2nd Circumference	6 4/8	6 3/8	1/8	11th Point		
3rd Circumference	6 5/8	6 7/8	2/8	12th Point		
4th Circumference	7 1/8	9 3/8	2 2/8	13th Point		
				Subtotals	10 4/8	26 7/8
Total	171 0/8	169 5/8	10 7/8	Total	37 3/8	

DATA		TOTALS	
Number of Points Right	9	Inside Spread	46 7/8
Number of Points Left	10	Right Antler	171 0/8
Total Nontypical	37 3/8	Left Antler	169 5/8
Tip to Tip Spread	47 4/8	Typical Gross Score	387 4/8
Greatest Spread	55 3/8	Difference	-10 7/8
Inside Spread	46 7/8	Typical Net Score	376 5/8
		Nontypical	+37 3/8
Gross Score	424 7/8	Nontypical Score	414 0/8

NUMBER 3 WORLD RECORD
ARCHERY
NONTYPICAL

P&Y 409 $^{0}/_{8}$

This article details the hunt for and harvesting of the No. 1 Pope and Young Montana nontypical elk. The elk is an 8x7 that green-scored 411 $^{6}/_{8}$ and has a spread of 62 $^{3}/_{8}$ inches. Its final score by panel measurement is 409 $^{0}/_{8}$.

This elk was taken on 26 September 1996 by Terry Crooks of Libby, Montana. His friend, Adrian Mathis, accompanied him and shared the joys of the event. The following account of the hunt is rendered from Terry's point of view and includes his thoughts and feelings at the time. He carries the reader through the events of that day step by step. The reader is there when the shot is made. Let's first look at some points of interest.

Any sightings of Crooks bull before the date of its harvest are sketchy. The only verifiable sighting was made by a lady who one day told a friend that she had seen a large bull elk with one antler. She was encouraged by the friend to go back and look for the missing antler, which might still have been in the area, and shortly she returned with a large nontypical drop that she had found.

Encouraged to return again to the area, she spent parts of the next two weeks looking for the other antler, hoping the bull had dropped the second one nearby. The second antler was recovered approximately one hundred fifty yards away. The antlers were then mounted with a cape. The taxidermist gave the rack an inside spread of 38 inches and rebuilt the first point, or eye guard, on the left side, which had been broken off. The remounted rack then measured 398.

For the next two years a small group of hunters kept the sheds a secret, hoping to find the bull themselves. Theories as to where the bull ranged and how big its tracks kept flying around. When the bull was finally harvested and its picture appeared in the local paper, the hunters who knew of the bull's existence finally knew the end of the story. The bull that had captured their imaginations was real, not merely dreamed of, and its green score of 411 $7/8$ confirmed their belief that it would soon be the new state record.

The Crooks bull's final Pope and Young and Boone & Crockett scores are different. The original dry score given for each was 407 $3/8$. In April of 1997, it was rescored by a Pope and Young panel in Edmonton, Alberta, and given the score of 409 $0/8$ P&Y. Although it was first thought that the head would be invited to be panel-scored by the Boone & Crockett committee, it was not, as 1997 produced an unusual number of outstanding bulls to score. Therefore, its final Boone & Crockett score has remained at 407 $3/8$.

The Crooks bull eclipses the former Montana state record archery nontypical Yellowstone elk by six points. That magnificent bull, scoring 403 $0/8$, was taken in 1987 by Donald Roberson and is available for viewing at the Jay Roberson taxidermy studio in Lincoln, Montana.

Terry Crooks, whose home is near Libby, Montana, is an accomplished bow hunter. Although Terry has taken many species of big game with his bow, elk are his predominant favorite.

Montana Nontypical State Record
by Terry Crooks

When the bull stopped in the opening at fifteen yards, it was like the replaying of a situation I had experienced and relived many times in my dreams. No shot was possible, but experience told me that this situation was going to change fast. There was a possibility the bull would escape our efforts. Like viewing pictures from an album, my mind whirled, assessing the possibilities from past experiences. Subconsciously, my mind had noted that this guy was big and had extra "trash" antlers hanging off at various angles. I couldn't study the rack during this flash encounter without risking being noticed or losing my focus on the task at hand. Never for a moment did I dream that before me stood the new Montana nontypical state record elk.

Once in a while, all hunters get lucky. We all hope for luck and even count on it sometimes, but it is said that "good hunters make their own luck." Over the years, I had missed several opportunities at great bulls. I have taken several good bulls, but in the alder-choked mountains of northwest Montana, where good hunters hunt all season or even several seasons in the hope of one good shot at a bull or a rare shot at a monster; missing can be something that haunts you for years. I wondered if it were possible that I would have such an opportunity again. *Maybe,* I thought, *I had run past all of my luck on the great bulls.* Despite all my worries and despite the difficulty of hunting elk in brush, I've always encouraged bowhunting by saying that "If we put in our time, one of us will win, and when one of us wins, we all win."

With that philosophy in mind, I confronted this giant bull. Somewhere behind me and downslope, my hunting partner, Adrian Mathis, stood frozen in a position that gave him less opportunity for a shot but a wide open view of the bull's massive rack. For a period of fifteen seconds, he memorized the points and was able to clearly establish the animal as a huge nontypical. Remaining motionless, he was content with his position and reasoned that if it was not his day to shoot, he hoped that somehow I would be able to take a shot.

With my sixty-five-pound Bear Kodiak recurve raised, I waited as time seemed to stand still. The aroma of the rut-crazed bull drifted over us, but still there was no possibility of a shot. Motionless, the bull stared down on us, unable to identify our camouflaged shapes.

The ritual that had brought us to this point in time began more than twenty years earlier. As teenagers, Adrian and I flung arrows together and dreamed of one day being able to effectively hunt big game with our bows. We had learned a lot and become pretty good with our bows by that special day, 26 September 1996, which started with a predawn march that soon demanded headbands on our sweaty foreheads. We carried in our packs the raingear needed to penetrate the brush without being drenched by the early morning dew. This morning, however, temperatures were below freezing and the dew was frozen on the brush. It left a white dusting of micro-ice on our clothing, but it quickly brushed off and spared us the drenching we'd expected to receive from the dew and the clammy sweat generated by the raingear.

After hiking approximately three miles in alder above our heads, we paused to adjust packs and sweatbands. Bugling into various basins brought no response, but when I changed the pace with a series of cow calls, a bull replied farther up the canyon. My partner had not heard it, and I questioned whether I actually had heard a response myself. We waited a few minutes and then called again, and a reassuring bugle came from a distance up the canyon.

We devised a plan to cut the distance to the bull. Earlier we had talked about one of us staying back and the other going in and trying to get a shot, but the intensity of the bull's bugling convinced both of us to go in. Approximately two hundred yards from the elk, we paused to talk strategy. After a quick exchange of elk talk, the bull came crashing down the mountain. We scrambled up the slope.

Every yard we gained gave us better odds that the elk would come past us and present a shot. At the same time, we were aware that our aggressive approach put everything at risk because if the elk caught us moving, he would freeze up and wait for identification or, worse yet, see us and be gone in an instant. After sprinting forward forty yards or so, I caught his movement above and to the left. I pushed as far as I could before freezing in shooting position just seconds before he stepped into the open.

Now, with the bull standing motionless before us, we waited for something to change. Would he turn and retreat when his bugles were not answered? We'd seen that before, and we could not answer him in this position. Would he crash past us or through us, thinking his objective was farther down the slope? We'd seen that before, too, and it wasn't a pretty picture, either. Would he slowly step forward, presenting a shot and giving a storybook ending to this event?

Our odds were going down with every moment—something needed to happen soon. Scanning the cover partly concealing the elk, I realized that the pine tree between us had a limb missing immediately over the vitals. I knew in an instant this was the shot that would have to be made. In one motion, I drew and released.

The arrow disappeared from sight, the bull lunged forward, and the yellow fletching quickly confirmed a solid hit close behind the front shoulder. The bull made a short dash through the brush, then all was silent. After a quiet conference, Adrian and I agreed that soon we would recover a lifetime trophy for both of us. We waited for an hour and then a second hour to make sure the arrow had done its work.

Shortly after picking up the blood trail, we found the bull in heavy brush sixty to seventy yards from where the arrow took him. All indications were that he had expired quickly.

After taking pictures, congratulating each other, and gasping at the size of the antlers, we began to bone and cape out the trophy. Adrian continued to remark about how massive the antlers were and that the only place he had seen anything of such size was at the Rocky Mountain Elk Foundation headquarters in Missoula. I was having a hard time believing any of it. I had seen the Elk Foundation exhibits but hadn't absorbed how big they were. Now before us was such an elk, and we had to figure out how to wrestle its antlers, cape, and meat out of the brush over the next couple of days.

Each step out was a major accomplishment. At times, Adrian would pull and I would push on the antlers to get them through the brush. We wondered how any animal could grow such antlers and live his life in such an alder-filled mess. We talked about leaving them behind—but only in jest, to relieve the frustration and danger of shoving a set of fifteen swordlike daggers through the brush. We never lost sight of the blessing we had received, and we were thankful even for all the bumps, bruises, and aching muscles received in the adventure.

The green score of the elk was 411 7/8, and the final score of 409 0/8 was awarded after the required panel scoring. This confirmed the head as the new Montana state Pope and Young record for nontypical Yellowstone elk.

In conclusion, I am still in awe that Adrian and I were blessed to share this hunt and its result. I am thankful that on that September day everything worked for us in a game plan that is usually controlled and won by the big bulls. We realized again that when one of us in the fraternity of elk hunters who sweat up and down the mountains wins, we all win! I am grateful to say that this elk belongs to all of us.

Terry Crooks with No. 3 archery nontypical.

NUMBER 3 WORLD RECORD ARCHERY NONTYPICAL

Year: 1996
Hunter: Terry V. Crooks

Location: Lincoln County, Montana
Owner: Terry V. Crooks

	Typical Points				Nontypical Points	
	Right Antler	Left Antler	Difference		Right Antler	Left Antler
Main Beam Length	54 7/8	53 5/8	1 2/8	1st Point	17 6/8	13 7/8
1st Point	17 1/8	16 5/8	4/8	2nd Point	6 3/8	
2nd Point	18 2/8	19 2/8	1 0/8	3rd Point		
3rd Point	21 4/8	22 3/8	7/8	4th Point		
4th Point	19 0/8	18 3/8	5/8	5th Point		
5th Point	13 4/8	10 2/8	3 2/8	6th Point		
6th Point				7th Point		
7th Point				8th Point		
8th Point				9th Point		
1st Circumference	8 4/8	7 5/8	7/8	10th Point		
2nd Circumference	7 2/8	6 6/8	4/8	11th Point		
3rd Circumference	6 7/8	6 3/8	4/8	12th Point		
4th Circumference	5 7/8	6 1/8	2/8	13th Point		
				Subtotals	24 1/8	13 7/8
Total	172 6/8	167 3/8	9 5/8	Total	38 0/8	

DATA			TOTALS	
Number of Points Right	8		Inside Spread	40 4/8
Number of Points Left	7		Right Antler	172 6/8
Total Nontypical	38 0/8		Left Antler	167 3/8
Tip to Tip Spread	34 3/8		Typical Gross Score	380 5/8
Greatest Spread	63 0/8		Difference	-9 5/8
Inside Spread	40 4/8		Typical Net Score	371 0/8
			Nontypical	+38 0/8
Gross Score	418 5/8		Nontypical Score	409 0/8

CHAPTER 29

NUMBER 4 MONTANA STATE RECORD NONTYPICAL

B&C 408 ^{4}/$_8$

The only time the Burlington Northern train whistles near Grant Garcia's Montana home is when animals are crossing the tracks to drink at the river. While out for a walk one week after he heard a whistle, Grant spotted an antler sticking out of the water. With help from his sons, he pulled the carcass to shore.

They theorize that the bull fell down the steep bank, broke its neck, and tumbled into the river. One of the bull's shed antlers from 1994 was found in the fall by a hunter, and the other side was discovered the next spring, several months after the bull had been found dead. Richard Hayes, an antler buyer, matched the sheds to the bull at a taxidermy shop.

1994 sheds.

Rich Hayes owns the bull's sheds from 1994, which look as if they would score about the same as the antlers found in 1995.

NUMBER 4 MONTANA STATE RECORD NONTYPICAL

Year: 1995
Found by: Grant Garcia

Location: Lincoln County, Montana
Owner: Grant Garcia

	Typical Points				Nontypical Points	
	Right Antler	Left Antler	Difference		Right Antler	Left Antler
Main Beam Length	50 $^7/_8$	47 $^1/_8$	3 $^6/_8$	1st Point	12 $^5/_8$	14 $^6/_8$
1st Point	15 $^3/_8$	13 $^7/_8$	1 $^4/_8$	2nd Point		
2nd Point	15 $^5/_8$	14 $^7/_8$	$^6/_8$	3rd Point		
3rd Point	16 $^0/_8$	13 $^4/_8$	2 $^4/_8$	4th Point		
4th Point	15 $^2/_8$	21 $^6/_8$	6 $^4/_8$	5th Point		
5th Point	17 $^0/_8$	20 $^0/_8$	3 $^0/_8$	6th Point		
6th Point	12 $^4/_8$	13 $^5/_8$	1 $^1/_8$	7th Point		
7th Point	4 $^0/_8$	7 $^6/_8$	3 $^6/_8$	8th Point		
8th Point				9th Point		
1st Circumference	8 $^5/_8$	9 $^5/_8$	1 $^0/_8$	10th Point		
2nd Circumference	11 $^5/_8$	8 $^4/_8$	3 $^1/_8$	11th Point		
3rd Circumference	7 $^1/_8$	7 $^4/_8$	$^3/_8$	12th Point		
4th Circumference	7 $^7/_8$	7 $^3/_8$	$^4/_8$	13th Point		
				Subtotals	12 $^5/_8$	14 $^6/_8$
Total	181 $^7/_8$	185 $^4/_8$	27 $^7/_8$	Total	27 $^3/_8$	

DATA		TOTALS	
Number of Points Right	9	Inside Spread	41 $^5/_8$
Number of Points Left	9	Right Antler	181 $^7/_8$
Total Nontypical	27 $^3/_8$	Left Antler	185 $^4/_8$
Tip to Tip Spread	36 $^4/_8$	Typical Gross Score	409 $^0/_8$
Greatest Spread	54 $^7/_8$	Difference	-27 $^7/_8$
Inside Spread	41 $^5/_8$	Typical Net Score	381 $^1/_8$
		Nontypical	+27 $^3/_8$
Gross Score	436 $^3/_8$	Nontypical Score	408 $^4/_8$

145

CHAPTER 30

NUMBER 5 MONTANA STATE RECORD NONTYPICAL

B&C 408 $^0/_8$

John Fitchett and his brothers grew up in a family of loggers. The boys were in the woods and mountains of Montana at a very young age, developing an intimate knowledge of and love for the outdoors and wildlife.

Hunting became a very important part of their lives when their father began to take them on pack trips back into the mountains.

One fall day, John and his younger brother, Brent, went after a big bull they had seen earlier. John was the successful hunter that day. A few years later, Brent shot a big bull with the same antler formation, perhaps a son of this bull.

NUMBER 5 MONTANA STATE RECORD NONTYPICAL

Year: 1980
Hunter: John Fitchett

Location: Sanders County, Montana
Owner: John Fitchett

	Typical Points				Nontypical Points	
	Right Antler	Left Antler	Difference		Right Antler	Left Antler
Main Beam Length	51 $^7/_8$	50 $^6/_8$	1 $^1/_8$	1st Point	4 $^0/_8$	3 $^0/_8$
1st Point	20 $^2/_8$	20 $^7/_8$	$^5/_8$	2nd Point		4 $^0/_8$
2nd Point	23 $^3/_8$	25 $^0/_8$	1 $^5/_8$	3rd Point		3 $^5/_8$
3rd Point	17 $^4/_8$	18 $^4/_8$	1 $^0/_8$	4th Point		
4th Point	21 $^4/_8$	21 $^6/_8$	$^2/_8$	5th Point		
5th Point	14 $^4/_8$	14 $^6/_8$	$^2/_8$	6th Point		
6th Point				7th Point		
7th Point				8th Point		
8th Point				9th Point		
1st Circumference	7 $^7/_8$	8 $^6/_8$	$^7/_8$	10th Point		
2nd Circumference	6 $^7/_8$	7 $^2/_8$	$^3/_8$	11th Point		
3rd Circumference	7 $^2/_8$	7 $^6/_8$	$^4/_8$	12th Point		
4th Circumference	7 $^2/_8$	6 $^7/_8$	$^3/_8$	13th Point		
				Subtotals	4 $^0/_8$	10 $^5/_8$
Total	178 $^2/_8$	182 $^2/_8$	7 $^0/_8$	Total	14 $^5/_8$	

DATA		TOTALS	
Number of Points Right	7	Inside Spread	39 $^7/_8$
Number of Points Left	9	Right Antler	178 $^2/_8$
Total Nontypical	14 $^5/_8$	Left Antler	182 $^2/_8$
Tip to Tip Spread	35 $^7/_8$	Typical Gross Score	400 $^3/_8$
Greatest Spread	48 $^0/_8$	Difference	-7 $^0/_8$
Inside Spread	39 $^7/_8$	Typical Net Score	393 $^3/_8$
		Nontypical	+14 $^5/_8$
Gross Score	415 $^0/_8$	Nontypical Score	408 $^0/_8$

CHAPTER 31

NUMBER 2 WYOMING STATE RECORD NONTYPICAL

B&C 406 $^2/8$

This is another great elk that we found in our travels. An elk hunter at a show said, "If you get to Lander, Wyoming, go into Warren and Jenny Spriggs's Fort Augur Trading Post."

Warren, who has a great collection of freak elk antlers, added this great nontypical to his collection some thirty years ago. As with a lot of the old trophies, hunter information has been lost with the years. The unique feature of this rack is that it has 69 $^4/8$ inches of nontypical measurement.

Jenny Spriggs holds the rack.

NUMBER 2 WYOMING STATE RECORD NONTYPICAL

Year: 1952
Hunter: Unknown

Location: Fremont County, Wyoming
Owner: Warren V. Spriggs

	Typical Points				Nontypical Points	
	Right Antler	Left Antler	Difference		Right Antler	Left Antler
Main Beam Length	49 4/8	49 6/8	2/8	1st Point	15 4/8	16 4/8
1st Point	15 4/8	15 5/8	1/8	2nd Point	7 1/8	2 6/8
2nd Point	13 7/8	16 3/8	2 4/8	3rd Point	12 4/8	8 0/8
3rd Point	18 6/8	16 6/8	2 0/8	4th Point		7 1/8
4th Point	17 4/8	20 6/8	3 2/8	5th Point		
5th Point	7 0/8	8 1/8	1 1/8	6th Point		
6th Point				7th Point		
7th Point				8th Point		
8th Point				9th Point		
1st Circumference	9 0/8	8 0/8	1 0/8	10th Point		
2nd Circumference	6 6/8	6 4/8	2/8	11th Point		
3rd Circumference	6 1/8	6 5/8	4/8	12th Point		
4th Circumference	7 2/8	7 0/8	2/8	13th Point		
				Subtotals	35 1/8	34 3/8
Total	151 2/8	155 4/8	11 2/8	Total	69 4/8	

DATA		TOTALS	
Number of Points Right	9	Inside Spread	41 2/8
Number of Points Left	10	Right Antler	151 2/8
Total Nontypical	69 4/8	Left Antler	155 4/8
Tip to Tip Spread	45 5/8	Typical Gross Score	348 0/8
Greatest Spread	58 6/8	Difference	-11 2/8
Inside Spread	41 2/8	Typical Net Score	336 6/8
		Nontypical	+69 4/8
Gross Score	417 4/8	Nontypical Score	406 2/8

NUMBER 2 MANITOBA NONTYPICAL

B&C 405 $^3/_8$

BY RANDY BEAN

December 6, 1986, was opening day of the first elk season for Manitoba's zones 23 and 23A (Riding Mountain area). The morning's frigid temperature of minus 30 degrees did not stop Ernie Bernat and his hunting partner, Terry Kilida; this day was allocated to their treasured hobby of elk hunting. Eight inches of new snow covered the ground and hoarfrost whitened the bushes, but there was very little wind, excellent conditions for the eager hunters.

After finishing the morning chores on their respective farms, which normally wouldn't have occurred until after sunup, Terry met Ernie at first light and they headed to their predetermined location. Upon arriving, they noticed that during the night some elk had stepped out and headed toward an alfalfa meadow located between two bluffs. Parking close to the first bluff, the two hunters prepared themselves for a stalk, hoping to catch a late-feeding bull or two.

The numerous sets of tracks leading onto the first bluff had the men's hearts racing. But when they reached the meadows moments later, their high hopes were dashed—no animals were feeding. Reassessing their plans and the area, they figured that Ernie should stalk through the bluff across the meadow and Terry should wait at the edge of the first bluff. Some tracks could be seen entering the second bluff.

Ernie had been on the bluff for only three to five minutes when a 6x6 bull appeared, walking toward the bluff on which Terry was standing. Terry made no mistake and collected a handsome 300-plus-point elk. Within minutes of the shot, game warden Terry Hoggins came by on a snowmobile and helped the pair move and load the elk. By 9 A.M. that year's hunt was a complete success! Little did they know there was more to come.

On their way home, pleased with the morning's hunt and full of praise for each other, the two enthusiastic hunters could not believe their good luck. Ernie's thoughts were jumping back to the scene of the hunt. *So many tracks and only one animal,* he thought. *Maybe . . .* As they hung and skinned the elk back at Ernie's farm, they were met by excited family members. Ernie began talking about going back to the site, giving the second bluff a good push and maybe coming up with a second elk. Terry agreed.

By 3 P.M. the two men were back at their hunting spot. This time they decided Terry would do the walking while Ernie watched the meadow—not from the first bluff but rather along the edge of the second. In the silent afternoon air Ernie heard a loud "snap," which caused him to jump and make a 180-degree turn. Saplings were breaking, lots of them, and the sounds were getting louder! Ernie's heart raced, and he thought, *This must be one heck of a huge animal.* He knew his first shot would be important, so he prepared his .30-06 and himself for the confrontation.

A bull broke from the bluff, and its size made Ernie's jaw drop. Never had he witnessed an elk so large, not in antlers but in body size. A giant! Though the bull was moving at good speed, it was able to discern Ernie's movements and veered to Ernie's right. But it was a good, open shot. While aiming, Ernie noticed the clearance between the snow and the animal's belly—never had he seen such a large elk. He just had to collect on this opportunity.

The monstrous monarch fell after only one shot, well placed in the left shoulder. It brought a sigh of relief from Ernie as he slowly lowered his rifle. Success! During a slow walk toward the fallen bull, Ernie thought of how proud this monarch must have been during his lifetime, a true Lord of the Woods. When Terry heard the shot, he rushed over to meet Ernie and confirmed that he, too, had never seen such a large-bodied elk.

The two of them could not possibly lift the huge elk, so they decided to find a third man to help. Within moments of a phone call, that help was ready to roll. The loading of the carcass from the ground to the bed of a half-ton truck took well over one hour. The three men finally accomplished the task by using ropes and working on sections of the carcass rather than the entire animal at once. Upon completing the formidable chore, the elk's rump was tight against the truck's cab window and the head and antlers had to be tied so they would not drag on the ground during the seven-mile drive home. This was one huge elk!

Ernie and Terry were mainly interested in the meat. Although they knew nothing about trophy competition, Jim Krosier of Dauphin advised Ernie to have the antlers scored. Today Ernie's massive elk rack stands as the No. 1 elk harvested in Manitoba with a score of 397 6/8.

Ernie later had me enter his trophy in the Boone & Crockett Club (I am an official measurer) competition for the 20th Awards period. Needless to say, Ernie's elk was invited to the 20th Awards display and panel measurement. His antlers arrived in Albuquerque, New Mexico, in late April of 1989.

On 1 January 1988 the Boone & Crockett Club began a new category: nontypical American elk. Now here is the twist: Ernie's elk was measured as a typical (no abnormalities), but there was one element that could be called abnormal. Ernie's elk was not the largest typical at Albuquerque, so the panel wondered: If we call this an abnormal, where would it place in the new category? Believe it or not, it placed 5th in the world, with a score of 405 3/8.

Because Ernie's elk would place higher in the Boone & Crockett book as a nontypical than as a typical—fifth as compared to about fortieth—Ernie and I opted for fifth place. The final typical score at the Awards was 395. I was surprised at the shrinkage of the beams. Each measurement had become 3/8 smaller, except one, which had become 4/8 smaller. The inside had changed by only 1 1/8.

NUMBER 2 MANITOBA NONTYPICAL

Year: 1986
Hunter: Ernie Bernat

Location: Vermilion River, Manitoba, Canada
Owner: Ernie Bernat

	Typical Points				Nontypical Points	
	Right Antler	Left Antler	Difference		Right Antler	Left Antler
Main Beam Length	59 4/8	58 1/8	1 3/8	1st Point	0	10 3/8
1st Point	17 2/8	18 7/8	1 5/8	2nd Point		
2nd Point	17 3/8	15 2/8	2 1/8	3rd Point		
3rd Point	18 0/8	17 1/8	7/8	4th Point		
4th Point	18 5/8	19 0/8	3/8	5th Point		
5th Point	15 4/8	14 1/8	1 3/8	6th Point		
6th Point	5 7/8	8 7/8	3 0/8	7th Point		
7th Point				8th Point		
8th Point				9th Point		
1st Circumference	8 4/8	8 2/8	2/8	10th Point		
2nd Circumference	7 4/8	7 5/8	1/8	11th Point		
3rd Circumference	7 7/8	8 3/8	4/8	12th Point		
4th Circumference	7 3/8	8 3/8	1 0/8	13th Point		
				Subtotals	0	10 3/8
Total	183 3/8	184 0/8	12 5/8	Total	10 3/8	

DATA		TOTALS	
Number of Points Right	7	Inside Spread	40 2/8
Number of Points Left	8	Right Antler	183 3/8
Total Nontypical	10 3/8	Left Antler	184 0/8
Tip to Tip Spread	35 4/8	Typical Gross Score	407 5/8
Greatest Spread	43 6/8	Difference	-12 5/8
Inside Spread	40 2/8	Typical Net Score	395 0/8
		Nontypical	+10 3/8
Gross Score	418 0/8	Nontypical Score	405 3/8

CHAPTER 33

WORLD RECORD
BLACK POWDER
NONTYPICAL

B&C 404 ¹/₈

Chris White spent the summer of 1993 scouting his Colorado hunting area for elk feeding and bedding areas. On 11 September, opening day of muzzleloader season, Chris and his hunting buddy, Paul Bianchi, were sitting at a fresh wallow waiting for daylight. In the excitement of the upcoming hunt, Chris had forgotten his bugle in the truck. Armed with a coyote call, he squeaked out a sound like a spike bull, then followed with some cow imitations. Immediately a bull responded, and for the next ninety minutes Chris worked the unseen bull.

Finally, Chris saw just enough antler to know it was a legal bull. When the elk closed to within fifty yards, Chris fired one shot from his CVA Frontier rifle loaded with a 490-grain patched round ball. The shot was good, and the trophy went only a short distance before lying down.

Buck fever set in and Chris began to shake as he approached the giant bull. The huge 9x7 would later be officially scored at 404 1/8 nontypical, a new world record for black powder.

Unknown to Chris, his neighbors, Jeff and Becky Barber, had photographed and videotaped the big bull the previous year. Jeff, who took the state record typical black powder elk in 1994, had also hunted Chris's bull in 1992.

In February, at the International Sportsmen's Exposition in Denver, both trophies were shown in the *Eastmans' Journal* elk display. The two hunters met there for the first time and started swapping stories. Chris saw the video and photos of his bull from 1992. Jeff and Chris had a great time sharing their stories with those who stopped by the booth.

After studying the 1992 photos of Chris's bull, I think it would have scored about the same then as it did when harvested. In 1992 the bull had longer brow points, shorter royal points, and one less nontypical point.

Chris White with world record black powder.

White's bull had been photographed alive the previous year by Becky Barber.

WORLD RECORD BLACK POWDER NONTYPICAL

Year: 1993
Hunter: Chris White

Location: Jefferson County, Colorado
Owner: Chris White

	Typical Points				Nontypical Points	
	Right Antler	Left Antler	Difference		Right Antler	Left Antler
Main Beam Length	51 6/8	52 5/8	7/8	1st Point	13 4/8	1 4/8
1st Point	15 6/8	14 2/8	1 4/8	2nd Point		12 1/8
2nd Point	18 6/8	18 4/8	2/8	3rd Point		6 6/8
3rd Point	24 0/8	19 6/8	4 2/8	4th Point		
4th Point	19 4/8	17 3/8	2 1/8	5th Point		
5th Point	13 6/8	15 2/8	1 4/8	6th Point		
6th Point				7th Point		
7th Point				8th Point		
8th Point				9th Point		
1st Circumference	9 7/8	10 1/8	2/8	10th Point		
2nd Circumference	7 0/8	7 0/8	0	11th Point		
3rd Circumference	7 4/8	7 5/8	1/8	12th Point		
4th Circumference	6 6/8	9 4/8	2 6/8	13th Point		
				Subtotals	13 4/8	20 3/8
Total	174 5/8	172 0/8	13 5/8	Total	33 7/8	

DATA		TOTALS	
Number of Points Right	7	Inside Spread	37 2/8
Number of Points Left	9	Right Antler	174 5/8
Total Nontypical	33 7/8	Left Antler	172 0/8
Tip to Tip Spread	37 4/8	Typical Gross Score	383 7/8
Greatest Spread	40 6/8	Difference	-13 5/8
Inside Spread	37 2/8	Typical Net Score	370 2/8
		Nontypical	+33 7/8
Gross Score	417 6/8	Nontypical Score	404 1/8

CHAPTER 34

IDAHO STATE RECORD NONTYPICAL

B&C 403 $^7/_8$

BY FRED S. SCOTT

It was October of 1964 in Shoshone County, Idaho. At four o'clock in the morning I was up, just like a lot of working people get into the habit of doing. I was trying to decide whether I should go elk hunting or just sit around the house all day. I couldn't go to work, as I had injured my left hand in an accident at the local silver mine where I worked. It was not possible to work in the dirty environment underground with an open wound because of the danger of infection.

It wasn't a hard decision; I decided on the elk hunt. It was just a matter of gathering the things I would need to take for a day of hunting: my rifle, ammo, bone saw, knife, rope, binoculars, lunch, and a pack to carry it all in.

I arrived at the trailhead at about 6 A.M., half an hour later than I'd hoped to get started. I was on Sunset Peak, which rises 6,424 feet. My plan for the early morning was to take the trail out to Pony Peak, then go around into the head of Pony Gulch, where I would hunt the water holes and wallows. In the afternoon I would move on to the Idaho Gulch side to hunt the bedding areas on the north slope of the main ridge. This would put me at approximately 4,000 feet in elevation. Come nightfall, I would have a good climb to get back to my vehicle.

I left Sunset Peak along a north-south ridge for the first quarter-mile, then turned off on the main east-west ridge. I was out on the main ridge about a quarter-mile, dogtrotting to make up for my late start, when a bull bugled just below the crest. I knew he had to be close, because I heard him clearly even with my hearing impairment. I stood real still, listening for the bull to bugle again. He did! I then realized that he couldn't be more than fifty yards away, and just out of sight. I bugled back at him, using a short squeal to make him think that I was a small bull that needed to be put in his place with a whippin'.

Up onto the ridge came a bull like nothing you have ever seen in your life, or I in mine. He looked like a cross between a caribou and an elk. He was broadside to me, hair standing on end, walking stiff-legged like they do when they are showing another bull just how "big and bad" they are. Posturing, I believe the game biologists call it.

The bull didn't see me as he crossed at about fifty yards, perfectly broadside. I dropped to the seat of my pants and held for a heart shot, right at the point of his "elbow." At the shot, the bull jumped forward and raked his antlers through a small evergreen on the ridge top. I shot again, with the same point of aim. He jumped again, turned to his left, and began to walk away. I aimed at his neck and shot for the third time. To my surprise, the bull continued over the side of the ridge and out of sight.

I could not believe this was happening! This would be my fifth elk, and all the others had dropped in their tracks with the first shot. What could be wrong? I was using a Model 721 Remington in .270 Winchester caliber, firing a handload that Jack O'Connor had recommended for elk. It was a 150-grain Nosler Partition bullet ahead of 59½ grains of Hodgdon 4831 military powder. This load gave an approximate velocity of 3,023 feet per second at the muzzle. With the rifle sighted dead-center at twenty yards, it was right on again at 275 yards, giving the hunter a simple, "dead-on" hold on shots out to 300 yards. Shooting my rifle from a benchrest, I could keep my shots in a six-inch bull's-eye at 275 yards. But not this time.

I knew I had a wounded bull on my hands. I checked the ground where the bull had walked off the ridge for signs of blood. There were just a few drops here and there. I started tracking him down the sidehill and over to a north-facing slope. Imagine, if you can, a hillside about as steep as the bottom half of a barn roof, covered with hemlock trees and an understory of huckleberry brush about chest high. That's right, I was in the "thick of things." Because the ground was covered with huckleberry leaves and other debris, it was difficult to follow the sign. I figured I would go until I lost the track or blood sign, then mark the spot and start making circles until I found another sign. I jumped the bull several times without seeing him. Finally, about the third or fourth time, I saw my elk. He was standing in a hole where an uprooted tree had left a deep depression.

The bull didn't jump or run, so I aimed to hit him under his ear. He was only fifty feet away! At the shot, I saw a piece of antler tine fly off his rack. This made me suddenly aware that my gun was not shooting where I was aiming it. Using some "Kentucky" windage and a whole lot of luck, I managed to hit my bull in the head and kill him (after two complete misses).

After I got over the excitement of the kill, I sat down for a smoke and a good look at this bull that I had just bagged. Boy, he had been in one hell of a fight—his shoulders and ribs were covered with scrapes and puncture wounds. Since then I have often wondered just how big the bull must have been that put such a whippin' on my big old bull. I estimated my elk to weigh about 900 pounds, about forty of that being the antlers. They were real heavy, with long tines and points going in every direction. Wow! There were nine points on each antler! This bull was certainly a trophy of a lifetime.

By this time, it was 10:30 A.M. This nice Indian Summer weather would get into the high 70s before the day was over. I would have to get the meat taken care of fast. It was hard to believe that I had been tracking this bull for more than 3½ hours. I field-dressed the elk without delay, then skinned and quartered him so I could get the meat off the ground. This allowed air to circulate around the meat and thus disperse the body heat faster. I hung the quarters from a tree, then sprinkled the moist areas with black pepper to take away the moisture that the blowflies would need to lay their eggs.

All these precautions were taken to ensure that I would have good-tasting meat the following winter, not just a freezer full of "wild meat."

After skinning the elk, I was able to determine where my bullets had hit. The first shot had hit right in the point of the brisket. The second went in under the near leg and shattered the other leg. This was probably what had caused the bull to turn left. The third shot hit in the left side of the neck, and my final shot hit the brain. I later determined that the problem with my shooting had been the reloads, which had been manufactured by a local gunshop. After pulling the bullets from the remaining cases, I found that there was a difference of up to fifteen grains of powder from one shell to another. This explained the different points of impact from one shot to the next. There also might have been just a touch of buck fever! This was the only time in thirty-five years of using handloaded rifle ammo that I have ever had such a problem.

With the meat taken care of, I had to get back to town and ready the horses to pack out my elk. By the time I arrived home, caught the horses, and saddled and loaded them on my truck, it was 3:30 P.M.

I drove around to the hotel where my brother, Don, lived and waited for him to come home from work. I wanted him to go with me, since he had always been a better packer and "rank-horse hand" than I. Besides, one of the horses I had loaded was Don's. Both of the horses were just starting to be trained to ride and pack. My brother's was a 4½-year-old Montana range horse of unknown breeding, and the other wasn't any better—a half-crazy, hot-blooded crossbreed of some sort that a friend had given me in hopes that I could calm it down to where someone could ride or pack it in safety.

We were just about to leave town when another friend, Frank, decided to come along for the ride. We arrived at Sunset Peak, unloaded the horses, and started down the trail without further delay. Don was in the lead, following the trail I had blazed on the way out. We were in a hurry to get the elk out before dark because the last quarter-mile up to the peak is a steep, narrow, rocky trail—not the best place to be with a green bronco after dark.

Once we got the elk, Don thought the quarters were covered with blowflies until he got a closer look and realized that it was just the black pepper I had put on them. We put the quarters in meat sacks, wrapped each in a canvas manta, and then loaded the quarters on the horses. Because of the excitable and unsteady nature of the horses, it was not practical to pack the antlers on them. It could easily have led to accident or injury to the horses or to us. Don and I would be occupied with handling the horses, so that left our friend Frank to pack the antlers. We padded the skull plate and antler bases well with our jackets, and Frank put them on his shoulders and followed the horses up the trail. We certainly wouldn't need our jackets on the steep climb back to the peak. We made it back to the truck and then on to town without incident.

Back in town, the antlers caused quite a stir. No one had seen antlers of this type before. Our local game warden, Wes McKeever, had been made aware of the kill, and he urged me to take the antlers to the regional office of the Fish and Game Department in Coeur d'Alene, Idaho, to have them measured for Boone & Crockett listing. The antlers were measured by Jack McNeel, regional public relations man for the department and also an official measurer for the Boone & Crockett Club. Both Wes and I were disappointed when the score of the unsymmetrical antlers was below the minimum necessary to make the record book.

Over the years, several different local business establishments have borrowed my antlers for display and several people have offered to buy them. Although I never thought there would be a nontypical elk class, I kept the antlers for my own satisfaction.

You can imagine my surprise when I received my Fall 1986 issue of *Bugle* magazine, published by the Rocky Mountain Elk Foundation, of which I am a member. This issue contained an article about the Boone & Crockett Club's consideration of starting a category for nontypical elk. The article requested that entries be made to establish whether there were enough trophies to warrant a nontypical elk class. I at once contacted Jack McNeel—yes, the same Jack McNeel who had measured them as "typical" twenty-two years earlier—to have him measure my antlers. Jack scored them this time at 401 2/8 points. The completed score chart was sent to Dr. Philip L. Wright, chairman emeritus of the Records of North American Big Game Committee, for his review.

In December 1986, the nontypical elk category was approved by the Records Committee. In February 1987, Phil Wright contacted me to get a remeasurement of the second tine on the right antler. In March of 1987, the Inland Big Game Council sponsored a Bighorn Show in Spokane, Washington. I entered the antlers in that show and they were given a score of 402 7/8. This score sheet was sent to Dr. Wright. After reviewing all the data, he sent in points to the club's office. The official entry scoring my elk was 403 7/8.

Thus ends my very nontypical elk story.

Originally published in the 20th Big Game Awards Book. *Reprinted with permission from the Boone & Crockett Club.*

IDAHO STATE RECORD NONTYPICAL

Year: 1964
Hunter: Fred Scott

Location: Shoshone County, Idaho
Owner: H&H Collection

	Typical Points				Nontypical Points	
	Right Antler	Left Antler	Difference		Right Antler	Left Antler
Main Beam Length	46 5/8	52 0/8	5 3/8	1st Point	20 4/8	15 6/8
1st Point	17 2/8	18 5/8	1 3/8	2nd Point	1 6/8	9 7/8
2nd Point	25 5/8	20 5/8	5 0/8	3rd Point		1 6/8
3rd Point	21 6/8	18 3/8	3 3/8	4th Point		
4th Point	19 3/8	21 3/8	2 0/8	5th Point		
5th Point	9 7/8	7 1/8	2 6/8	6th Point		
6th Point				7th Point		
7th Point				8th Point		
8th Point				9th Point		
1st Circumference	10 3/8	10 6/8	3/8	10th Point		
2nd Circumference	8 4/8	8 1/8	3/8	11th Point		
3rd Circumference	8 3/8	7 4/8	7/8	12th Point		
4th Circumference	6 3/8	5 4/8	7/8	13th Point		
				Subtotals	22 2/8	27 3/8
Total	174 1/8	170 0/8	22 3/8	Total	49 5/8	

DATA		TOTALS	
Number of Points Right	8	Inside Spread	32 4/8
Number of Points Left	9	Right Antler	174 1/8
Total Nontypical	49 5/8	Left Antler	170 0/8
Tip to Tip Spread	29 6/8	Typical Gross Score	376 5/8
Greatest Spread	43 5/8	Difference	-22 3/8
Inside Spread	32 4/8	Typical Net Score	354 2/8
		Nontypical	+49 5/8
Gross Score	426 2/8	Nontypical Score	403 7/8

CHAPTER 35

NUMBER 2 WASHINGTON STATE RECORD NONTYPICAL

B&C 401 $^5/_8$

A hunter brought this elk to a taxidermist in Washington State to be mounted. While in the shop he told his story of how he had shot the elk near Mount St. Helens. The hunter never returned to claim his mount.

The elk was displayed in the shop for twenty-four years until the taxidermist retired in 1983. It was subsequently purchased by Steve Crossley and hung in his meat store for the next fifteen years. It is now in the Bass Pro Wildlife Museum in Springfield, Missouri.

An old metal antler tag reads, "1959 Y.I.R. Elk #304." Maybe it refers to the Yakima Indian Reservation.

The old mount before I remounted the head.

NUMBER 2 WASHINGTON STATE RECORD NONTYPICAL

Year: 1959 Location: Mt. St. Helens area, Washington
Hunter: Unknown Owner: Bass Pro Wildlife Museum

	Typical Points				Nontypical Points	
	Right Antler	Left Antler	Difference		Right Antler	Left Antler
Main Beam Length	53 ⁵/₈	55 ⁵/₈	2 ⁰/₈	1st Point	13 ⁰/₈	17 ³/₈
1st Point	16 ¹/₈	16 ²/₈	¹/₈	2nd Point		15 ³/₈
2nd Point	13 ⁶/₈	12 ⁶/₈	1 ⁰/₈	3rd Point		
3rd Point	12 ²/₈	12 ⁷/₈	⁵/₈	4th Point		
4th Point	23 ⁶/₈	25 ⁶/₈	2 ⁰/₈	5th Point		
5th Point	16 ⁵/₈	11 ¹/₈	5 ⁴/₈	6th Point		
6th Point				7th Point		
7th Point				8th Point		
8th Point				9th Point		
1st Circumference	7 ⁷/₈	7 ⁴/₈	³/₈	10th Point		
2nd Circumference	7 ⁰/₈	7 ⁰/₈	0	11th Point		
3rd Circumference	6 ⁷/₈	8 ⁵/₈	1 ⁶/₈	12th Point		
4th Circumference	7 ⁰/₈	5 ²/₈	1 ⁶/₈	13th Point		
				Subtotals	13 ⁰/₈	32 ⁶/₈
Total	164 ⁷/₈	162 ⁶/₈	15 ¹/₈	Total	45 ⁶/₈	

DATA		TOTALS	
Number of Points Right	7	Inside Spread	43 ³/₈
Number of Points Left	8	Right Antler	164 ⁷/₈
Total Nontypical	45 ⁶/₈	Left Antler	162 ⁶/₈
Tip to Tip Spread	40 ⁷/₈	Typical Gross Score	371 ⁰/₈
Greatest Spread	51 ³/₈	Difference	-15 ¹/₈
Inside Spread	43 ³/₈	Typical Net Score	355 ⁷/₈
		Nontypical	+45 ⁶/₈
Gross Score	416 ⁶/₈	Nontypical Score	401 ⁵/₈

CHAPTER 36

OREGON STATE RECORD
NONTYPICAL
ARCHERY

P&Y 400 ⁰/₈

Bill Hamilton hunted a new area in 1980, saw a lot of bulls, and shot a nice five-point. It was not until 1982 that he and his wife, Marjorie, returned to hunt that canyon again. Bill was up the first morning bugling and put a few stalks on raghorns, but no luck.

The next day was Bill's "bowhunt of a lifetime." He headed to the spot where the bulls had been the night before and started glassing. Three different herds could be seen above the timber. Bill knew his best chance was to get below them and wait for the elk to drop back into the timber. He found a good spot and bugled. The mountains came alive—elk above, elk below, elk all around him. He was ready. Three small bulls filed by at forty to fifty

Bill Hamilton holding his trophy's antlers.

yards—no shots. Cows and calves went by at ten yards. An hour went by as elk were bedding all around.

Two bulls were at a wallow about eighty yards below. Bill wanted one of them, so he started sliding down the hill on his butt. He was pinned down, cows all around, so he decided to bugle. The herd exploded and headed for the high country—going, going, gone. *What the heck?* he thought, and bugled again, but they didn't stop.

What an adrenaline rush! He sat down and took a deep breath. Out of the corner of his eye Bill saw a huge bull get up out of its bed and look downhill. Bill drew his bow back and started to turn toward the bull. Swinging past its head, all he could see were antlers. All those missed shots of the past filled his head—*Please, not now,* Bill thought, and released the arrow. The bull exploded in a sideways, swirling, uphill run with dirt flying everywhere. It was a good shot, and the bull went down after sprinting about seventy-five yards.

Bill sat down and watched—the mountains went still as if nothing had happened. He walked up to the big animal and began counting points. Wow, 12x8—what a trophy!

OREGON STATE RECORD NONTYPICAL ARCHERY

Year: 1982
Hunter: Bill Hamilton

Location: Wallowa County, Oregon
Owner: Bill Hamilton

	Typical Points				Nontypical Points	
	Right Antler	Left Antler	Difference		Right Antler	Left Antler
Main Beam Length	55 1/8	53 0/8	2 1/8	1st Point	13 0/8	13 2/8
1st Point	15 6/8	16 0/8	2/8	2nd Point	3 4/8	
2nd Point	16 5/8	17 1/8	4/8	3rd Point	3 4/8	
3rd Point	13 6/8	21 0/8	7 2/8	4th Point	3 6/8	
4th Point	21 0/8	12 4/8	8 4/8	5th Point		
5th Point	16 4/8	14 0/8	2 4/8	6th Point		
6th Point	1 6/8	14 3/8	12 5/8	7th Point		
7th Point	2 2/8	0	2 2/8	8th Point		
8th Point				9th Point		
1st Circumference	9 0/8	10 0/8	1 0/8	10th Point		
2nd Circumference	7 6/8	7 7/8	1/8	11th Point		
3rd Circumference	8 2/8	7 6/8	4/8	12th Point		
4th Circumference	8 6/8	10 1/8	1 3/8	13th Point		
				Subtotals	23 6/8	13 2/8
Total	176 4/8	183 6/8	39 0/8	Total	37 0/8	

DATA		TOTALS	
Number of Points Right	12	Inside Spread	41 6/8
Number of Points Left	8	Right Antler	176 4/8
Total Nontypical	37 0/8	Left Antler	183 6/8
Tip to Tip Spread	31 6/8	Typical Gross Score	402 0/8
Greatest Spread	51 3/8	Difference	-39 0/8
Inside Spread	41 6/8	Typical Net Score	363 0/8
		Nontypical	+37 0/8
Gross Score	439 0/8	Nontypical Score	400 0/8

CHAPTER 37

THE GREATEST ELK

B&C 398 ³/₈

This great elk was donated to the National Collection of Heads and Horns (Boone & Crockett Club) around 1910 by Mrs. Archibald Rogers. The skull was cleaned and displayed as a European mount until 1996, when I had it mounted for the World Record Elk Tour. On tour for three years, this elk was the most looked at, photographed, and talked about head of any elk that I am aware of, aside from the John Plute bull. Thus I name it The Greatest Elk.

In 1998, while lying in bed in a motel room somewhere and reading *Boone & Crockett Records of North American Big Game* (1939 Edition), I found the name Colonel Archibald Rogers. It described how he took a 7x7 bull in the Wind River Range of Wyoming, date unknown. Farther along in the book his name again appeared, this time for taking a grizzly bear at Greybull River, Wyoming, in 1890.

This prompted me to start looking for information in Wyoming as we traveled through that state. In the spring of 1998, we were scheduled for a show in Buffalo, Wyoming. We had a few days off and time to investigate.

We went to the Buffalo Museum, and what did I find but a picture of Colonel Archibald Rogers and a display of his Indian artifacts. The museum director told me that Rogers's sister had lived near Buffalo for many years and that the family owned a ranch near Meeteetse, Wyoming.

It was another year before I had a chance to stop in Meeteetse. I visited the museum and bought a book there titled *Brand of A Legend: Ten Thousand Years in the Valley of the Greybull River—Archaeology, Plains Indians, Outlaws, Ranchers, and Wildlife*, by Bob Edgar and Jack Turnell.

Archibald Rogers, an easterner who had an interest in the Bar T L Ranch, wrote a story for *Scribner's Magazine* about a hunting trip on the Greybull River in 1883. The following pieces from this article reflect some of the game conditions in the Greybull River country at that time.

Rogers, after getting back to Wyoming from the east, describes the last portion of the trip, which I received permission to reprint.

However, we have no time to linger and, picking our way among the countless buffalo wallows which indent the level surface of the summit, the wagon, with wheels double locked, is soon groaning and creaking down the descent (Meeteetse Rim), which leads to the merrily rushing Meeteetse, which we follow down to its junction with Greybull. We are then inside our own fence and are joyously welcomed by the dogs. Here, too, I find my trusty friend and companion of all my hunting trips, Tazwell Woody, a grizzled veteran of the mountains. From the ranch to the mountains is a comparatively short trip, for one day's travel to the westward would place you well on their slopes.

Let me say of this portion of the range, that it is the most rugged, broken, and precipitous of its whole extent and the charm of overcoming its apparent inaccessibility can only be appreciated by one who has toiled and sweated in surmounting the difficulties of mountain travel from a pure love of nature in its wildest and grandest form.

In another portion of the article, Rogers wrote:

Reader, what would you have given to have seen, as I have, a band of 250 bull-elk all collected together on a beautiful piece of green grassy turf at an elevation of 9,000 feet? Here was a sight to make a man's nerves tingle. This was the largest band of bulls, by actual count,

Original European mount.

Unique mount showing all the antler features.

that I have ever seen, though my cousin and partner once saw, in the fall of the year, including bulls, cows, and calves, fifteen hundred.

Rogers killed several elk, mountain sheep, and bears on this hunt. The antlers of one of the elk heads measured 49 inches across and 64 inches long. Rogers stated that:

Bear seek their winter quarters in the badlands and in the mountains. Those that adopt the former come out much earlier; consequently, if the hunter is on the ground soon enough, he may, by beginning in the lower lands first and working toward the mountain be reasonably sure of securing good skins as late as June. One will, of course, occasionally see a very large skin and from its size it would seem impossible that the animal that once filled it out could have weighed less than 1,200 pounds. But I think that it is safe to say that most specimens that one will get in the mountains will be under, rather than over 500 pounds. Colonel Pickett, who has a neighboring ranch, and who has killed more bear than any man I know of, weighed his largest, which, if I remember rightly, weighed 800 pounds.

Colonel Rogers lived in Hyde, New York. Back in the late 1800s, animals were being collected for the National Museum. Colonel Rogers's 7X7 bull from Wyoming is listed as the world record in the 1939 Boone & Crockett book. This is the same bull Colonel Rogers wrote about on his hunt in 1883.

I am sure this freak elk, having such abnormal antlers, was met with great interest. The bull was not listed in the early record books, which recorded animals by the length of the largest antler.

THE GREATEST ELK

Year: Late 1800s
Hunter: Colonel Archibald Rogers

Location: Possibly Wyoming
Owner: Boone & Crockett Club
Natl. Collection of Heads & Horns

	Typical Points				Nontypical Points	
	Right Antler	Left Antler	Difference		Right Antler	Left Antler
Main Beam Length	43 ³/₈	45 ⁵/₈	2 ²/₈	1st Point	13 ⁰/₈	13 ¹/₈
1st Point	12 ⁴/₈	11 ⁷/₈	⁵/₈	2nd Point	6 ⁴/₈	8 ⁰/₈
2nd Point	12 ³/₈	12 ⁵/₈	²/₈	3rd Point	14 ⁵/₈	12 ⁴/₈
3rd Point	18 ³/₈	17 ⁴/₈	⁷/₈	4th Point	12 ¹/₈	4 ⁰/₈
4th Point	14 ⁰/₈	15 ²/₈	1 ²/₈	5th Point	4 ⁰/₈	8 ¹/₈
5th Point				6th Point		6 ⁵/₈
6th Point				7th Point		
7th Point				8th Point		
8th Point				9th Point		
1st Circumference	9 ¹/₈	9 ⁰/₈	¹/₈	10th Point		
2nd Circumference	7 ¹/₈	7 ⁰/₈	¹/₈	11th Point		
3rd Circumference	7 ³/₈	8 ⁶/₈	1 ³/₈	12th Point		
4th Circumference	8 ⁰/₈	5 ⁷/₈	2 ¹/₈	13th Point		
				Subtotals	50 ²/₈	52 ³/₈
Total	132 ²/₈	133 ⁴/₈	9 ⁰/₈	Total	102 ⁵/₈	

DATA		TOTALS	
Number of Points Right	10	Inside Spread	39 ⁰/₈
Number of Points Left	11	Right Antler	132 ²/₈
Total Nontypical	102 ⁵/₈	Left Antler	133 ⁴/₈
Tip to Tip Spread	37 ⁴/₈	Typical Gross Score	304 ⁶/₈
Greatest Spread	47 ⁶/₈	Difference	-9 ⁰/₈
Inside Spread	39 ⁰/₈	Typical Net Score	295 ⁶/₈
		Nontypical	+102 ⁵/₈
Gross Score	407 ³/₈	*Nontypical Score	398 ³/₈

*Not officially entered in records at this date.

CHAPTER 38

NUMBER 12 MONTANA STATE RECORD NONTYPICAL

B&C 394 $^3/_8$

Gerald Small is an elementary school teacher on the Rocky Boy Indian Reservation in north-central Montana. At every opportunity he is out hunting, hiking, and enjoying the outdoors. "This keeps me in shape," he said. In the spring he looks for shed antlers. On one of those trips, he spotted the white tips of some antlers sticking out of the grass. Upon further investigation, Gerald found the whole rack and skeleton of this great bull. The cause of death was unknown. After carrying the heavy antlers out, he decided to weigh them—an impressive 44 pounds.

Gerald Small and Don Stemler holding the head.

NUMBER 12 MONTANA STATE RECORD NONTYPICAL

Year: 1990
Found by: Gerald Small

Location: Hill County, Montana
Owner: Gerald Small

	Typical Points				Nontypical Points	
	Right Antler	Left Antler	Difference		Right Antler	Left Antler
Main Beam Length	55 5/8	49 7/8	5 6/8	1st Point	8 6/8	2 2/8
1st Point	16 2/8	16 1/8	1/8	2nd Point		
2nd Point	18 5/8	18 2/8	3/8	3rd Point		
3rd Point	22 0/8	26 2/8	4 2/8	4th Point		
4th Point	18 0/8	20 0/8	2 0/8	5th Point		
5th Point	13 7/8	13 0/8	7/8	6th Point		
6th Point	8 1/8	0	8 1/8	7th Point		
7th Point				8th Point		
8th Point				9th Point		
1st Circumference	9 7/8	9 6/8	1/8	10th Point		
2nd Circumference	8 7/8	8 5/8	2/8	11th Point		
3rd Circumference	8 1/8	7 5/8	4/8	12th Point		
4th Circumference	9 1/8	7 1/8	2 0/8	13th Point		
				Subtotals	8 6/8	2 2/8
Total	188 4/8	176 5/8	24 3/8	Total	11 0/8	

DATA		TOTALS	
Number of Points Right	8	Inside Spread	42 5/8
Number of Points Left	7	Right Antler	188 4/8
Total Nontypical	11 0/8	Left Antler	176 5/8
Tip to Tip Spread	39 4/8	Typical Gross Score	407 6/8
Greatest Spread	47 3/8	Difference	-24 3/8
Inside Spread	42 5/8	Typical Net Score	383 3/8
		Nontypical	+11 0/8
Gross Score	418 6/8	*Nontypical Score	394 3/8

COLORADO STATE RECORD NONTYPICAL ARCHERY

P&Y 389 $^5/_8$

BY MARK MARTIN

Several years ago, I hunted exclusively with a rifle and scope. Then I started using a little lever-action .30-30 without a scope. From there, my choice of weapons evolved to handgun, then muzzleloader, and finally to the bow. I've always been able to sneak up on animals, and I enjoy the challenge of a primitive weapon.

I always take the month of September off to hunt, but last year I kind of goofed off, spending the first part of the season filming with my video and still cameras. During that time, I was so close to elk that I nearly got stepped on, and more than once, I had to get out of the way of their antlers. I took over a thousand photos and got some beautiful shots.

I knew before the season there were big bulls in my chosen area because I pick up shed antlers almost every weekend. I pursue that hobby all over the state, and that's usually how I decide where I'm going to hunt. The quality of the sheds is a good indicator of the quality of bulls in an area.

One morning I was sitting on a ridge looking down about four hundred yards, when I heard two big bulls bugling. They were deep, mature bugles. When the pair came out into a clearing, one of them was the bull I eventually killed, and the other was every bit as big, if not bigger. The other bull probably would have scored better because the bull I harvested had broomed eight inches off his first brow tine. My bull would have grossed 413 if not for that.

At first, the bulls just bugled at each other across the meadow for about fifteen minutes. Then they moved closer together, sizing each other up. The two elk then turned and kind of pointed their antlers toward each other and paced back and forth, eying one another. It was the greatest thing I've ever seen in my life!

The bulls would move to opposite ends of the meadow and bugle at each other, then turn and walk back toward one another. I thought I was going to see a great fight, but not once did they lunge at each other. They finally stopped and seemed almost to back away from each other. Neither one turned his back. I'd never seen that behavior before. I decided right then and there that it was time to put the cameras away and do some serious hunting.

That day, lots of cows and bulls were in the area, and I ended up having satellite bulls trailing me. Because I use so much elk urine, I always have to watch my back because young bulls will follow my every step, almost like a dog. Thanks to the satellite bulls coming in and a bunch of wild turkeys messing me up, it wasn't a very productive day. Everything seemed to go wrong.

I had my outfitter's pack loaded with enough supplies to spend the night, so I just stayed right there in the thick of things. With the bulls bugling and racks clicking and rattling all night, I didn't get much sleep.

The next morning, I got up on the larger of the two big bulls, which by then had thirty to forty cows with him. They hadn't moved more than four hundred yards overnight. It was fairly breezy, and I spent most of that morning just trying to get into position.

At one point, about 2 P.M., the elk bedded down out of the heat in the shade of some trees. I thought I had a real good chance to make a stalk on that big bull, so I sprayed myself really good. It sounds bizarre to most people, but when I'm moving in on a bull, I completely soak my bandanna with cow-in-heat urine.

Then I tie it up over my face, bank-robber style. I feel this is necessary because I take my time and crawl almost halfway into the herd. I'm right in among them.

The elk got up to feed, and my assault didn't work out, because the satellite bulls were constantly bugling and coming in, only to be chased off by the big bull. He finally scurried his cows up into the brush just a little too quickly for me to get a shot. I was probably within sixty yards, but had I knelt up to draw, I'd have been spotted. It was time to head back to camp for more food.

On 13 September, I headed in a different direction and ran into the bull that I eventually harvested. It was late morning, and the elk had stopped responding to my Scheery cow call, so I was using the Hyper Hot and Lonesome Cow calls. After watching a couple of cows being bred, I knew why the big bulls weren't responding. They were busy breeding.

Moving in on the herd, I came to a clearing and got set up in a draw ahead of them. I was using the Scheery just to let them know something was over there. Then I'd hit the Lonesome Cow call, relaxing the cows as they came into the draw. The bull was coming to me perfectly about sixty yards out. Suddenly, the cows spun and ran back, and the bull spooked. I thought they had caught my wind, and I was trying to figure out what I'd done wrong when a sow bear and two cubs came out of that draw. I had to quickly backpedal up into the timber to make sure I got out of their way.

The elk moved over two draws, so I stayed in the brushy timber, dodging small bulls and little groups of cows as I moved in on the big bull again. Finally, I caught his herd in a tiny washout basin. I got all urined up and soaked my bandanna, tying it in place around my face.

Once again I worked my way into the herd. The satellites kept circling and the big bull became uncomfortable, moving his cows 150 yards to a clearing. I've found that big bulls like to keep their cows in the open, when they can keep an eye on them and don't have to worry about a satellite bull cutting out any of the harem.

The big bull was constantly bugling as I made my stalk. The herd was moving away, so I hit the Hyper Hot call. It didn't seem to affect the cows, but the bull turned, looked back in my direction, and bugled. I grabbed my Power Bugle and hit a perfect note. He ran at me for about thirty yards, bugling with his head tipped back. He jumped into some brush and was thrashing it when I hit the Lonesome Cow call one more time. He was interested in what was back there, but I wasn't able to draw him in.

For a while we played the game where he bugled and then I bugled. Rubbing some brush down low where he couldn't pinpoint my location, I bugled, then hit the Hyper

Hot. Man, he was positive there was a cow ready to breed! He came running in, looking around and bugling, trying to get a response.

Finally, he stepped into a spot where he had no view of me and I could draw. All the while, he was urinating and bugling, trying to find out where the cow was. He stepped out just far enough to give me a perfect broadside shot and started bugling again.

I don't know whether he saw me, but he kind of turned his head in my direction. The bull was only twenty yards away, and the one thing I remember is that his nose was flared almost inside out. Things seemed to go into slow motion as I released the arrow and watched it strike perfectly. When the arrow hit, the bull spun and took off running into the brush. I knew I had a good hit, so I bugled and cow-called a little to calm him down. Once he went into the brush, I knew it was just a matter of time. For about an hour I sat there reviewing the whole scenario of the shot. When you're in a situation like that, you get impatient and think an hour has gone by when it's only been ten minutes. With barely enough light left to see, though, I knew I'd better get to tracking.

There was lots of blood where he'd been standing when I hit him. Fifty yards farther into the brush, I found the fletching end of my arrow. I ended up using my flashlight, and it took what seemed like half the night to finally find him.

When I walked up on him, I just sat there, savoring the moment. Exhausted, I curled up beside the giant bull and napped for a while before taking care of him. I wasn't about to leave him there overnight.

The next morning, I began the five-mile pack to the truck, where I always keep large coolers filled with blocks of ice. You have to be careful at that time of year, for warm weather can easily spoil your cape and meat. After several trips, I finally had everything back to the truck and safely on ice.

Author's Note: Mark's bull, net-scoring 389 5/8 P&Y, is the new Colorado state record archery nontypical.

Mark Martin holds his rack.

COLORADO STATE RECORD NONTYPICAL ARCHERY

Year: 1998

Location: Douglas County, Colorado

Hunter: Mark Martin

Owner: Mark Martin

	Typical Points				Nontypical Points	
	Right Antler	Left Antler	Difference		Right Antler	Left Antler
Main Beam Length	52 4/8	54 0/8	1 4/8	1st Point	4 3/8	12 0/8
1st Point	13 4/8	14 0/8	4/8	2nd Point		
2nd Point	17 3/8	18 2/8	7/8	3rd Point		
3rd Point	17 2/8	17 2/8	0	4th Point		
4th Point	22 6/8	22 4/8	2/8	5th Point		
5th Point	19 2/8	16 3/8	2 7/8	6th Point		
6th Point				7th Point		
7th Point				8th Point		
8th Point				9th Point		
1st Circumference	8 4/8	8 1/8	3/8	10th Point		
2nd Circumference	6 7/8	6 6/8	1/8	11th Point		
3rd Circumference	7 0/8	7 2/8	2/8	12th Point		
4th Circumference	7 4/8	7 3/8	1/8	13th Point		
				Subtotals	4 3/8	12 0/8
Total	172 4/8	171 7/8	6 7/8	Total	16 3/8	

DATA		TOTALS	
Number of Points Right	7	Inside Spread	35 6/8
Number of Points Left	7	Right Antler	172 4/8
Total Nontypical	16 3/8	Left Antler	171 7/8
Tip to Tip Spread	25 6/8	Typical Gross Score	380 0/8
Greatest Spread	45 5/8	Difference	-6 7/8
Inside Spread	35 6/8	Typical Net Score	373 2/8
		Nontypical	+16 3/8
Gross P&Y	396 4/8	Nontypical Score	389 5/8

CHAPTER 40

NUMBER 7 WYOMING STATE RECORD NONTYPICAL

B&C 389 ⁴/₈

It was late in the 1961 season when Lester Beydler headed to the mountains west of Buffalo, Wyoming. After shooting a giant bull, he started tracking the wounded animal. When dark set in, the hunt was halted until the next morning. Lester awakened to a blizzard covering his tracks and all sign of the elk. Winter had set in. It was a long one for Lester, who spent much time thinking about the big bull. Losing an animal is a hunter's worst nightmare.

The following summer, Lester found the bull's remains, including the rack, which he put on his barn.

Years later the antlers were given to Arlan Tift, who bolted them to the front of his realty business in Buffalo, Wyoming. They hung there for years

I measure the rack on the front of the realty building in Buffalo, Wyoming.

until Don Stemler and I happened to drive by. Don spotted the rack. After parking the truck and trailer we borrowed a ladder for a rough measurement. Wow—another record elk! A smaller set of antlers has replaced the rack on the realty business. I had this bull mounted for Arlan, and it was displayed on the World Record Elk Tour.

NUMBER 7 WYOMING STATE RECORD NONTYPICAL

Year: 1961
Hunter: Lester Beydler

Location: Johnson County, Wyoming
Owner: Arlan W. Tift

	Typical Points				Nontypical Points	
	Right Antler	Left Antler	Difference		Right Antler	Left Antler
Main Beam Length	47 3/8	50 4/8	3 1/8	1st Point	4 6/8	5 0/8
1st Point	17 6/8	19 0/8	1 2/8	2nd Point	13 0/8	13 6/8
2nd Point	20 5/8	22 4/8	1 7/8	3rd Point	3 1/8	
3rd Point	18 0/8	16 5/8	1 3/8	4th Point		
4th Point	17 5/8	16 0/8	1 5/8	5th Point		
5th Point	12 3/8	7 1/8	5 2/8	6th Point		
6th Point				7th Point		
7th Point				8th Point		
8th Point				9th Point		
1st Circumference	8 4/8	8 4/8	0	10th Point		
2nd Circumference	6 5/8	6 5/8	0	11th Point		
3rd Circumference	6 4/8	6 4/8	0	12th Point		
4th Circumference	7 5/8	6 3/8	1 2/8	13th Point		
				Subtotals	20 7/8	18 6/8
Total	163 0/8	159 6/8	15 6/8	Total	39 5/8	

DATA		TOTALS	
Number of Points Right	9	Inside Spread	42 7/8
Number of Points Left	8	Right Antler	163 0/8
Total Nontypical	39 5/8	Left Antler	159 6/8
Tip to Tip Spread	43 4/8	Typical Gross Score	365 5/8
Greatest Spread	64 2/8	Difference	-15 6/8
Inside Spread	42 7/8	Typical Net Score	349 7/8
		Nontypical	+39 5/8
Gross Score	405 3/8	Nontypical Score	389 4/8

CHAPTER 41

WORLD RECORD FIVE-POINT NONTYPICAL

B&C 386 $^5/_8$

Tom Satre and his good friend, Marvin Craver, headed up a Montana mountain to hunt a favorite alpine basin. Soon, two five-point bulls came out of the aspens, and several shots were fired, downing both animals. The hunters ran up to the two elk and just stood there. In all the excitement, they were not sure who had shot which bull.

After some friendly argument, the animals were skinned and the bullet was removed from the larger of the two bulls. The slug was from Tom's .264 and so he earned credit for tagging the bull.

This great elk has five typical points on each antler and one nontypical point off of the left side by the fourth point. Two outstanding features on this bull are its 30-inch third points and 26-inch fourth points. The rack has the highest typical score for a basic five-point, measuring 383 $^4/_8$ inches.

Hunter and owner Tom Satre holds the rack of the world record five-point nontypical: B&C 386 5/8.

WORLD RECORD FIVE-POINT NONTYPICAL

Year: 1966
Hunter: Tom Satre

Location: Gallatin County, Montana
Owner: Tom Satre

	Typical Points				Nontypical Points	
	Right Antler	Left Antler	Difference		Right Antler	Left Antler
Main Beam Length	44 6/8	46 1/8	1 3/8	1st Point		10 3/8
1st Point	19 6/8	18 0/8	1 6/8	2nd Point		
2nd Point	22 1/8	23 5/8	1 4/8	3rd Point		
3rd Point	29 2/8	30 1/8	7/8	4th Point		
4th Point	25 5/8	26 0/8	3/8	5th Point		
5th Point				6th Point		
6th Point				7th Point		
7th Point				8th Point		
8th Point				9th Point		
1st Circumference	9 6/8	9 6/8	0	10th Point		
2nd Circumference	7 3/8	7 5/8	2/8	11th Point		
3rd Circumference	7 0/8	7 7/8	7/8	12th Point		
4th Circumference	5 4/8	5 2/8	2/8	13th Point		
				Subtotals		10 3/8
Total	171 1/8	174 3/8	7 2/8	Total	10 3/8	

DATA		TOTALS	
Number of Points Right	5	Inside Spread	38 0/8
Number of Points Left	6	Right Antler	171 1/8
Total Nontypical	10 3/8	Left Antler	174 3/8
Tip to Tip Spread	38 2/8	Typical Gross Score	383 4/8
Greatest Spread	44 4/8	Difference	-7 2/8
Inside Spread	38 0/8	Typical Net Score	376 2/8
		Nontypical	+10 3/8
Gross Score	393 7/8	Nontypical Score	386 5/8

CHAPTER 42

WORLD RECORD
ROOSEVELT ELK
SHEDS

B&C 429 $^4/_8$

Harold and Belva Burroughs, who live in Molalla, Oregon, about thirty miles southeast of Portland, came to the International Sportsmen Exhibition in Portland to see the great elk on display. Belva told me about the big set of sheds they had found, as big as any trophy in my display. Several weeks later they brought the sheds to the Northwest Trails show in Pendleton, Oregon, for me to measure. Later, Fred King from Montana Fish, Wildlife and Parks, an official measurer for Boone & Crockett and the Shed Record Book, and I panel-measured the sheds and determined them to be the new world record Roosevelt.

These antlers adorned the greatest Roosevelt elk ever. In the current record book, the world record scores B&C 388 and No. 2 scores B&C 384. When we

Sheds of the big Roosevelt, left to right: 1986, 1988, 1990.

mounted the sheds, we used a 39-inch inside spread (40 inches is quite common in the Roosevelt elk). The rack gross score was a whopping B&C 431 0/8 inches, *43 inches larger than the world record.* It is hard to believe this animal lived a good share of its life just thirty miles away from one million people.

This largest set of sheds was found in the spring of 1990 by Harold Burroughs and his son-in-law, Sam Aho, about one hundred yards from the house of Ron DeRoche, Harold's other son-in-law. The thirty feet of barbed wire wrapped around the antlers made finding the pair quite easy.

The bull was well known in the area—other neighbors had found earlier sheds and had photographed and videotaped the bull itself. The sheds from 1986 scored B&C 384 7/8, and the 1988 set scored B&C 378 3/8. The bull had been seen wintering in the area for some eight years, with the last sighting having occurred in the spring of 1994. The 1994 set scored B&C 386 6/8. We guessed its age at thirteen to fifteen years.

At the 1999 Rocky Mountain Elk Foundation convention in Portland, Oregon, all four sets were on display side by side. As you can see from the scores, that bull's antlers varied by only about four inches during most of its adult life, but the 1990 set zoomed up to B&C 431. The conditions of food, water, and minerals that year must have been ideal and readily available for this great elk.

ROOSEVELT SHEDS - 1986 SET
OWNER: SHAWN WHITE
SCORES: 384 7/8 "

1986 sheds. Owner: Shawn White.

ROOSEVELT SHEDS - 1994 SET
OWNER: REED & SHIRLEY JOHNSON
SCORES: 386 ⅝ "

1994 sheds. Owners: Reed and Shirley Johnson.

The trophy Roosevelt bull. Clackamas County, Oregon, 1988. (Photo by Larry Wrolstad.)

WORLD RECORD
ROOSEVELT ELK SHEDS

Year: 1990
Found by: Harold Burroughs & Sam Aho

Location: Clackamas County, Oregon
Owner: Harold & Belva Burroughs

	Typical Points				Nontypical Points	
	Right Antler	Left Antler	Difference		Right Antler	Left Antler
Main Beam Length	52 4/8	50 5/8	1 7/8	1st Point	1 7/8	
1st Point	18 3/8	20 0/8	1 5/8	2nd Point		
2nd Point	19 0/8	17 7/8	1 1/8	3rd Point		
3rd Point	19 6/8	16 3/8	3 3/8	4th Point		
4th Point	19 0/8	20 1/8	1 1/8	Crown Points		
5th Point	17 0/8	17 0/8		1st Point	3 2/8	14 6/8
6th Point	4 0/8	0		2nd Point	8 5/8	7 1/8
7th Point				3rd Point		8 3/8
8th Point				4th Point		
1st Circumference	9 5/8	9 1/8	4/8	5th Point		
2nd Circumference	8 1/8	8 1/8	0	6th Point		
3rd Circumference	8 5/8	8 3/8	2/8	7th Point		
4th Circumference	8 6/8	9 0/8	2/8	8th Point		
				Subtotals	11 7/8	30 2/8
Total	184 6/8	176 5/8	10 1/8	Total	42 1/8	

DATA		TOTALS	
Number of Points Right	10	Inside Spread	38 0/8
Number of Points Left	9	Right Antler	184 6/8
Total Nontypical	1 7/8	Left Antler	176 5/8
Total Crown Points	42 1/8	Crown Points	+42 1/8
Tip to Tip Spread	Unknown	Typical Gross Score	441 4/8
Greatest Spread	59 0/8	Difference	-10 1/8
Inside Spread, Estimated	38 0/8	Typical Net Score	431 3/8
		Nontypical	-1 7/8
Gross Score	441 4/8	Typical Score	429 4/8